WHAT OTHER MILLENNIALS ARE SAYING ABOUT *CAREER HACKING FOR MILLENNIALS:*

"Max's advice can be followed by almost anyone in almost any profession. This is the guidebook I wish I had when I was 19 and starting out at Google. From working in corporate to building a startup, *Career Hacking for Millennials* would've saved me from learning the hard way, time and time again."

FALON FATEMI, *Google's youngest employee at 19. Co-founder and CEO of Node.io, backed by Mark Cuban and others.*

"*Career Hacking for Millennials* is jam-packed with actionable advice that everyone building a career should read, no matter how far along they are. We're purchasing books for our entire company, because I know every employee will be better off personally and professionally for having read it."

BRYCE MADDOCK, *co-founder and CEO, TaskUs, an industry-leading business process outsourcing firm with nine-figure revenues.*

"We interview hundreds, if not thousands, of millennials each year for new hires at Mulesoft. Now I might be able to speed these up by asking just one question, 'Have you read *Career Hacking for Millennials?*' This book has the answers I've spent time and energy learning over the past decade and will certainly put any reader well ahead of their peers."

STEVEN BROUDY, *former US Army Special Operations Team Leader and current Director of Inside Sales at Mulesoft, from pre to post IPO.*

D0816412

"I've always looked to Max as an innovator in his career, from what he's done with Sales Hacker to investing to travel and more. In this book, he does a great job of cutting straight to the point and preparing the reader with creative and practical ways to create a successful career."

JUSTIN MARES, *co-founder and CEO of Kettle and Fire Bone Broth and Perfect Keto, and author of the bestselling book,* Traction. *Sold his first tech company to Rackspace.*

"I felt like I lived every word as I went along. There are so many learnings perfectly summarized, I just wish it existed ten years ago!"

BEBE CHUEH, *former lawyer who sold her first tech company to LegalZoom. Now co-founder of Atrium with Justin Kan of Justin.tv.*

"It's never too late to focus on your career. *Career Hacking for Millennials* is a book I wish I had when I was graduating from college, and one that I will give to my kids when they do the same, regardless of their industry or profession."

MELISSA WASSER, *former Vice President at Goldman Sachs and current Director, Head of Private Capital Markets, Financial Technology Partners.*

"People often ask me for career advice. I'm glad I have something tangible to refer them to from now on. Reading this book will put you far ahead of the pack."

TAWHEED KADER, *Global Vice President of Strategy and Corporate Development, Marketo. Youngest vice president within the $30 Billion Portfolio of Vista Equity Partners.*

Career Hacking for Millennials

Max Altschuler

ISBN: 978-0692065655

TABLE OF CONTENTS

"I do all this for work-life balance. For fulfillment. And because I really like to build companies. Some people watch movies. Some play golf. I build companies, live a healthy lifestyle, and explore the world doing it."

-MAX ALTSCHULER

Introduction

MY STORY

Being a Millennial

There are more than 80 million of us. We were born between 1982 and around 2004, and handed this label: "millennial." And while we may love it, hate it, or just ignore it, the workplace doesn't. To succeed in your career, you need to know the challenges and opportunities that come from being a part of this generation. And that starts with a look at how we were raised.

It's not just about the technology or pop culture we grew up around. One of the defining characteristics is that many of us had helicopter parents—overprotective, excessively involved, and trying to solve all of our problems.

For me, this became clear in fifth grade, when my mom took me to the doctor to get an Adderall prescription and see if I had a diagnosable learning disability. Apparently, I was having trouble learning like the other kids.

I remember the day. I was playing kill the man with the ball, a game played almost like it sounds, during our post-lunch recess. I tackled another kid and felt my right middle finger bash against his head. I continued playing anyway, fueled by adrenaline.

When my mom picked me up, I jumped in the car and showed her the injury. "I think I broke my finger," I told her.

"Oh no, we've waited months for this doctor's appointment," she replied without looking. "You're not getting out of it that easily." We had met with other specialists before, and she thought I was trying to weasel out of another appointment.

"Um, ok," I responded.

After a 30-minute drive and three hours of board games, tests, and questions, we walked out of the office and back into her car. "Mom, can we go to the doctor now?" I asked. "Look at my finger."

She was mortified. It was so swollen, it looked like a bratwurst the color of an eggplant.

We drove to the hospital. When a doctor finally looked at my finger, he said, "This looks like it's been broken for awhile. Why didn't you come right over?!" My mom was in tears.

Karen Altschuler was an amazing mother, who always wanted the best for me. But that day, in that moment, she was a classic millennial mom, wanting to fix everything and give me the easiest paths possible—in this case through medicine, special classes, anything.

She didn't want to accept that I might be different. That things might be harder for me in some ways. She took a long-term view, believing that "fixing" how I learned would ensure that I could one day go to college and have a successful career. She was so caught up in thinking this way that she was neglecting what really was wrong and needed to be fixed right then, my broken finger. She was focused on the future. I was living in the now. And the future wouldn't turn out the way she feared.

This is the environment a lot of us grew up in. If you can relate, this book is for you.

I soon stopped taking the Adderall because it crushed my creativity. I was put into some special remedial classes, which I hated. But they didn't make much difference, and I still got by with Cs. I did OK on my SATs with a 1200 out of 1600 and got into the schools I wanted to go to.

I majored in architecture, simply because it was the only class I had done well in throughout high school. It took until my senior year for me and everyone around me to realize I'm a hands-on learner. I needed to learn by *doing* and *experiencing*. By trying, failing, and then succeeding.

Why am I telling you this? Because it set the stage for my journey to becoming a successful entrepreneur, investor, and advisor. To the first time my bank account hit the million-dollar mark.

More importantly, I've had the chance to become a well-rounded human being by figuring things out on the fly.

With this book, I'm passing along the lessons I learned the hard way, working for startups, starting multi-million dollar businesses, investing in more than 40 companies with a total valuation well into the billions, traveling to more than 80 countries, running and speaking at international conferences in front of 5,000+ attendees, and writing the bestselling book *Hacking Sales*. I've had the chance to reach tens of millions of people worldwide.

My goal is to share things you'll absolutely need to know in order to follow your own path. We'll go over everything from building your personal brand to cutting your teeth to finding mentors, setting yourself up for a killer career and healthy lifestyle.

I don't claim to have all the answers. No one does, and no book does. So throughout this book, I've drilled down on areas in which I do have expertise. It's packed with the kind of advice I've given people to help them successfully hack their careers. Along the way, I'll also be sharing some quotes and ideas from my experienced network of friends.

While I wrote this aimed at the millennial and Gen Z generations, it should be applicable to anyone. I want to help create a world and workforce that is flexible, adaptable, and aims to get the most out of everyone. No matter who you are, consider this your handy career guide.

Thinking Like an Entrepreneur

In my elementary school, we had a little Student Store where we could buy supplies. Parents would give their kids a few dollars if they needed a new binder or some pencils.

One year on Halloween, I went trick or treating and landed a huge score. My parents, of course, did not want me eating all that candy quickly, so they put it on top of the refrigerator. Over the next few weeks, I would climb up on the counter when they weren't looking and grab handfuls of candy. Most kids might sneak back to their room and eat away. I brought the chocolate bars, fun-size Skittles, and other candies to school in my backpack and sold them to classmates. They paid with the money they were supposed to spend on school supplies.

My dad still tells the story, with pride, of the day he got a call from the principal's office, detailing my venture. I was an entrepreneur from the beginning. My father's son. He's run a one-man-show financial advisory practice my entire life.

I always found odd ways to make money throughout my childhood and teenage years. When I was in middle school on Long Island, Pokemon became big. I never cared about the phenomenon, but spotted a business opportunity. I would buy packs of Pokemon cards for $3.99 and memorize the values. I'd use that knowledge to trade up with people, convincing them to swap their more expensive cards for my cheaper ones. Most kids didn't know the values, they just knew the characters.

I'd also play basketball games in which the winner got cards. Then I'd bring the cards I collected to flea markets and sell them there. I'd end up with anywhere between $20 and $80 per card.

I used the money to buy one of the first computers that had a CD burner. Using Napster, I'd burn CDs (yes, I downloaded music illegally as a kid, as did millions of others in my generation), then sell those CDs in the school hallways.

I didn't waste the money. My dad taught me all about saving. I had a little brown safe with a rotating dial at home and would keep it in there. Every time I had more than $1,000, I'd give the money to my dad, and he would put it away for me.

These early experiences were crucial. They taught me the ropes of business, the challenges and opportunities, and the importance of saving.

Even if you didn't learn this as a kid, you can now. Consider experimenting with something small, just to get the hang of it. Create a product, and sell it on Etsy or eBay or to your friends and contacts over Facebook. Find the pricing sweet spot.

Learn what people want and need, and how you can provide that with goods or services. Don't pressure anyone to buy anything, just keep evolving what you do until you find what works and makes people happy. Don't worry at first about turning it into a big business. Learn the fundamentals of entrepreneurship just like a kid would—by doing. And when you make money, save it to invest in your own future, your own next idea.

Doing this will help you learn a lot about business. You'll see why people say to "sell the sizzle, not the steak"—meaning turning your business into a story or idea that excites people. You'll learn about validating your ideas with customer reviews, pre-selling, making landing pages that work, targeting customers over Facebook, and lots more.

This process will also help you discover things about yourself. You'll see which aspects of business come easily to you and which require more work. And you'll see that with courage, stamina, commitment, and a willingness to learn, you can go a long way. Then you can take your efforts to the next stage.

For me, the next stage came when I moved from New York—the only home I'd ever known—to Arizona, where I'd experience my first big failure. I wouldn't trade that experience for the world.

From College to the Real World

I went off to college at Arizona State, getting as far away from the cold as possible. For the first three years, I had a lot of fun, but also blew some precious time. I was sputtering around, not knowing what I would do with my life. My interest in architecture was still strong, but the housing market crashed, and I knew there would be no jobs for me when I graduated if I continued in the field. I needed to switch.

In my senior year, I had an inspiration to start a bike share program (like CitiBike, before it existed). Two friends and I applied for a grant competition through the university. We won $2,500 to get started—very little, but enough to spark the fire. Most importantly, the grant gave us some credibility at the university.

To give the business as close to my full attention as possible, I reorganized my life. I changed my major to a bachelor's of interdisciplinary studies, which allowed me to combine courses from different fields. It's also known as a BIS, with the nickname "barely in school." I figured out that with this major, only half my college credits had to be in person and at ASU. So I applied to as many online courses as I could and courses at local community colleges, which were much cheaper.

I would get the syllabus the first week of class, then spend the next week completing all of the online assignments. I put the assignment due dates on my Google calendar, so I could simply press a button to have my work turned in on those days, and my semester was done. This freed up my time to focus on the bike share program while finishing my degree.

Over the following year, my friends and I secured a contract for exclusive rights to commercial bike sharing at the school. The university architect signed off on locations for the bikes to be placed.

We had meetings with the surrounding cities and transportation officials. We were hopeful.

But we still needed to raise money for the bikes and bike racks, and to cover expenses like power, insurance, and marketing. It was 2009, when the United States was grappling with the Great Recession. No one was giving three 22 year olds in Arizona a million dollars for an on-campus bike share program.

So we were out of luck. Without funding to help us take off, we had to give up. It stung. It was failure on a larger scale than I'd ever felt before.

But it turned out to be good medicine. Looking back, I'm glad we weren't able to raise the money. We learned a ton from this about gauging a market, understanding how the big-picture economy can impact an idea, and more. We had also underestimated the amount of work it would take. That bike-sharing business would have been a pain in the ass, with legal and insurance liabilities left and right.

I graduated from college just as the business was failing. I had no job lined up and a so-so degree. And the recession had made finding work very tough. At the same time, I had a friend with knowledge of affiliate advertising, in which companies pay game developers or bloggers—usually per click or per sign up—to advertise their products and services. It was thriving despite the recession. Companies in the space were getting fresh venture funding, and industry conferences were growing. My friend's brother worked for an up-and-coming company in the space, so we were able to leverage some of his knowledge and connections.

Social media advertising revenue was also starting to take off, so we decided to try to build viral applications to generate revenue from the affiliates. At the time, anyone could build an app inside Facebook. New traffic from affiliates, consumers, and businesses was funneling in that direction. Companies like Candy Crush were making millions.

We built a meme generator, but didn't know enough about how to make something go viral. Then we tried to build a better RSS reader (which aggregated your favorite blog articles), but we didn't understand user behavior well enough to create a better product. As hard as we tried and as much as we researched, we couldn't figure out a way to build a great, original app that would succeed on Facebook.

So we pivoted. We started a business helping small business owners leverage Facebook for lead generation and advertising. We focused on prospects such as bars, restaurants, and real estate agents—business folks who were trying to use social networks to advertise 24/7, but didn't know how. At that time, Facebook was able to act as your business website, yellow pages, social network, and penny-saver newspaper.

In our first week, we closed a $5,000 deal. In our first two months, we closed $25,000 in new business and had a pretty good pipeline built. We were reaching out actively to our networks, and our pipeline for potential business looked good. We brought another friend onto the team. We were working out of my apartment in Arizona through the end of my lease, chugging sugar-free Redbull and 5-Hour Energy drinks by the package.

We began talking about how, since our business was online, we could do it from anywhere. We discovered that we all had a dream of building a business while running it from another country. What better time than now, we thought.

It made business sense too. We could live somewhere much cheaper than the U.S. and get more mileage out of our revenue. Of course, we'd have to set up somewhere with reliable WiFi and electricity, and around the same time zones as the U.S. for customer communication.

So we packed our bags and headed off. We spent a few months in Playa Hermosa, Costa Rica, followed by San Juan Del Sur, Nicaragua. Each month, we closed a few more deals and made enough to survive in Central America. We lived near a beach for quick and easy surf breaks, worked by pools, and filled our days with rich coffee, fresh fish tacos, and cold beer.

We were learning and doing pretty well. But we were also making all kinds of mistakes. We weren't charging nearly enough for our services. We weren't clearly defining what we'd do for our clients, so expectations were off. We had a few clients who took advantage of our inexperience by asking for revision after revision of our work. We also had a habit of selling a feature or service and then figuring out how to develop or deliver it afterwards. We needed the revenue and irrationally thought we'd be able to quickly outsource some elements while still making a profit. It always worked out, but caused a ton of unnecessary stress and urgency.

Finally, we faced the facts. This life was fun, but if we wanted to build something big, we needed to go work for companies and proven executives from whom we could learn. This is an essential lesson. In your early years in business, soak up knowledge. The stories of some kids right out of college creating billion-dollar businesses are famous because they're so rare. Those stories often involve luck and connections, along with skills and great ideas. And sometimes, even the young people who create those don't know how to run them for long, because they haven't learned business basics.

So to learn, grow, and build a career, I started applying for jobs. I even made my resume into an infographic using an Upwork designer, so I could stand out from the crowd. It only cost me $30.

I wanted to work for a startup that I was passionate about. And for me to have a shot at getting hired with what little experience I had, there would have to be an opening for an early sales or business development hire. I studied what was out there, made my top picks, and reached like crazy for some jobs I probably wasn't qualified for but was confident I could succeed in.

I also had a few backups in mind—or so I thought. Two of my backups were Yelp and Demandforce. They seemingly hired anyone with a pulse right out of college, and I at least had some relevant experience. I didn't get either job.

I still remember the names of the recruiters who turned me down. Fear was setting in. I wasn't getting the jobs I was reaching for, or they weren't moving through the process very quickly. Getting rejected from what I thought were backups felt like a safety net for my future being taken away.

My number one choice was Udemy, a startup that made teaching and taking online courses available to everyone. In 2011, the education market was valued at over two trillion dollars. Having just been through college on the backend of a recession, I knew how massive the opportunity could be to provide people with skill-based courseware at a relatively low price compared to other education models. The company also had well-known, early-stage investors, which was good signaling and a testament to the capabilities of the founders. The timing, market size, and team seemed perfect for me.

I flew to San Francisco and went through seven hours of interviews with Udemy over the course of two consecutive days. About a week passed by with no word from them. Then, finally, the call came that I was hired. I was relieved and elated.

I promised myself two things. First, I would never be in this position again—jobless, scared, and feeling that I had no control over my immediate future. And second, I would do everything I possibly could to succeed at this job. When you get a shot, you shoot the shit out of it. You make it count.

I was hired as the first Sales/Business Development employee and second overall business employee behind the VP of Marketing. They needed someone who had the entrepreneurial traits to build without any hand holding. Who would just make stuff happen. Someone with the experience to run a full sales process competently. So, they decided to give me a chance.

I built out the supply side of the Udemy marketplace and helped steer the company through its seed, Series A, and Series B rounds of funding. When I started, we were onboarding five high quality rated courses per month. By the end of my second month, I had redesigned our sales process. I also redefined what "a high quality course" consisted of, making it a tougher designation, but began onboarding over 50 high quality courses per month.

Over the next few months, I negotiated contracts with three of the largest publishers in the world, Pearson, O'Reilly, and Wiley; secured our first paid partner deal in higher education with the University of Cincinnati; and worked with 32 other publishers to onboard their course catalogues. We sped past our main competitor, who had rejected me. I admit, that felt great. Udemy is now worth over a billion dollars. That feels even better.

I left Udemy when I felt my learning plateau. We had gone from a small, scrappy startup to an established company. My day-to-day impact on the business was decreasing as we hired out. I felt it was time to move on to a new learning experience. So I went to a small bootstrapped company called AttorneyFee to manage business development.

I worked hard and fast—and soon we were acquired by LegalZoom. It was a good story for the resume and a good learning experience, but it was almost too fast. I didn't want to work for a large corporation, nor did I want to move to their new headquarters in Austin, Texas. So I moved on again.

I had no idea what I wanted to do next. But I knew I had learned enough working for other people, and I was done making other people rich. It was my turn to own the big chunk of equity.

While I was at Udemy and AttorneyFee, companies would come to me to ask for my feedback on building repeatable and scalable sales processes. I was constantly getting hit up by companies to talk to their sales teams and advise them. I usually said yes, because I was interested in the networking and it's always good to help when you can. Especially in your industry. Through those interactions, I ended up meeting some brilliant tech sales leaders working on sales problems that we all found fascinating.

So I started a small and invite-only meetup and called it The Sales Hacker Meetup. We met once per month, and everyone brought something new and unique to the table.

We happened to have a meeting a few days after I left AttorneyFee. I announced that I'd like to start a conference focused on the kinds of things we discussed at our meetups. I said maybe we'd have 100 people, and that I'd find some sponsors to cover the costs.

It took me just six weeks to organize the first conference, which ended up having 300 people pay and sign up, plus a few big sponsors paying over five figures each. That's how Sales Hacker started. It was a conference, and I had no intention to turn it into a company.

In fact, I launched the company because I had to. A corporate sponsor wanted to pay $10,000, but I couldn't take it as a personal check. We needed to look like an established company. So I went out, started the LLC, and opened a bank account. At the end of that first conference, I had $60,000 in profits—after just six weeks of work.

I went full time on it, officially becoming a founder. At Sales Hacker, we've gone on to build a community of tens of thousands of sales professionals. We've partnered with more than 100 companies, including giant public corporations such as LinkedIn, Salesforce, HubSpot, Adobe, and more. We've organized conferences and meetups for thousands of attendees every year, across five continents.

The success of Sales Hacker has given me the chance to help start two other multimillion-dollar media companies, CMX Summit and SaaStr; become an adviser and investor; start a business for a healthy coffee alternative called SUTRA; and have all kinds of adventures.

All of this is possible because of the techniques I've learned to hack a career. Structural, pragmatic lessons. Things you need to know to give yourself every opportunity for success. That's what this book is for—to give you the lessons and guidance I didn't have, making your path a lot easier and quicker.

I'm not a genius. I didn't go to an Ivy League school, nor did I have family in the industry or funding me along the way. I'm pretty much a normal guy—but one who is good at self-reflecting, analyzing my situation, and finding hacks to get ahead.

How to Use This Book

Consider this a handy guidebook, written in bite-sized increments to help you make maximum use of your time. Keep it on your desk and refer back to it whenever you face a new task, from sending a cold email to whipping up a presentation. Most important of all, keep in mind the broad lessons. This is not a how-to-get-a-job book, although advice in here will help you accomplish that. It's a how-to-build-a-career-book.

There's a lot in here about how to handle the challenges and struggles you'll face, including self-doubt and sensitive interactions in the workplace. There are also a lot of actionable tips, tactics, and strategies to help you hack your career and improve yourself in the process.

Here's how to build the network, expertise, and reputation to conquer your career your way.

Section I

STARTING ON A CAREER PATH

If you don't know what you want to do with your life, you're not alone. You're never too old to be lost, and you're only truly in trouble if you're not trying new things. That's the key: to keep trying until you figure it out.

I knew I was entrepreneurial, but had no idea where my career would take me. I just tried a lot of different things and eventually found my direction. You will too. I've met plenty of people who've started out drastically differently from where they are now. I have a good friend who was an industrial engineer for almost a decade before she decided to go into tech.

Keep iterating, keep exploring, and don't be afraid to take one step backwards in order to take two steps forwards. It's never too late to find your true calling. Your career is long, and it may change. Heck, some of the largest companies in the world were all created by founders over the age of 40, like Home Depot, Gap, Intel, IBM, and many more.

What to Look for When Choosing a Company

Your 20s are for learning, your 30s are for earning.

At the start of your career, focus on learning over salary. You'll be way better off for it. This is not the time to be impatient. It's your time to start heavily investing in *transferable assets*—things like skill sets, deep relationships, social networks, and your personal brand. These things will move with you and compound over your career, making you more money and bringing you further in the long term.

The fact that I spent my 20s focusing on learning, rather than trying to amass a big wad of cash, is largely responsible for the successes I've had. And it's not just me. Tim Ferris, author of *The 4-Hour Workweek*, says the same thing. "It often comes down to prioritizing skill acquisition over immediate, post-college earning," he told *Time*, noting that a lower-paying job in your 20s can lead to making much more in your 30s.

Being a good learner is more important than ever in today's business environment. When a University of Phoenix survey asked people across the workforce to choose the most important skills evaluated in new hires, they placed "the ability and willingness to learn new skills" at the very top, with 84% calling it "very important." So in your 20s, double down on learning. You're less likely to have other responsibilities, like supporting children or a family yet.

To do this right, I recommend getting rid of unnecessary habits like video games or Netflix series. Or, at least, limit your time on those things and be regimented about it. This is precious time—don't waste it. *The Chicago Tribune* says "an unusually large percentage of able-bodied men, particularly the young and less-educated, are either not working or not working full-time," partly because they're spending so much time on video games. And *PC Magazine* says people are wasting an hour a day just searching for stuff to watch on Netflix. That hour—let alone the time spent watching the actual programs—could be put toward learning job skills.

Use your time wisely to get ahead. Remind yourself, constantly, that great accomplishments don't just happen. They come from learning, practicing, and growing. When Michael Jordan hit a game-winning three-pointer at the buzzer, it wasn't the result of work done in seconds. It was due to work done years earlier, getting coached and spending tons of time on the practice court, shooting 50 times from the same spot, seven days a week, for a decade.

It's the time you put in during practice that prepares you for the game. Your 20s are your practice time. So look for companies that will give you the greatest opportunities to learn and grow. Companies that are optimal for making you better in the long term. Look on lists like the Inc 5000, Entrepreneur 360, and others to find fast-growing and innovative companies to apply to.

What to Look for When Choosing a Boss

It's not just about the company. It's also, perhaps more so, about the people. Who would your boss be? What can he or she teach you? What about their boss, and onward up the chain to the company leadership? When considering possible employers, learn everything you can about these people. Study their successes and failures. Be sure they have relevant experience in a space that interests you. Read any posts they've written online. Look on their LinkedIn profiles for what other positions they've held and what kind of recommendations they've received.

Chinese business magnate Jack Ma says the chance to get hands-on learning from an excellent boss is a big reason you should consider working for a small company. "Normally in a big company it's good to learn processes. You're a part of a big machine. But when you go to a small company, you learn the passion, you learn the dreams, and you learn how to do lots of things at any one time. So before 30 years old, it's not which company you go to, it's which boss you follow. It's very important. A good boss teaches you differently."

A good way to find out about the company and the boss or bosses you'd report to comes in job interviews. Keep in mind that you get to ask questions as well. Ask about learning, mentorships, and access to executives. If you're going to give blood, sweat, and tears to the company, make sure you're getting the education you deserve. Asking about this can really impress interviewers. They want employees who are looking to grow and be engaged in self-improvement.

Today's forward-thinking companies also know that opportunities to learn and grow are particularly important for millennials.

Gallup found that 87% of people in our generation rate "professional or career growth and development opportunities" as important to them in a job. Sixty-nine percent of other workers say the same. This also means that other workers in our generation are focusing on learning—so if you don't, you'll lose out to the competition down the road. Don't let that happen.

Failing to put real thought into learning opportunities is easily the biggest mistake I see people make in choosing a job. There's no substitution for working for someone you can learn from. It should also be someone who has your back, has firm footing at the company, and has a network you can tap into.

Optimizing Your LinkedIn Profile

Having a LinkedIn profile is crucial in jump starting and building a career. As I write this book, I have about 20,000 LinkedIn followers who view my posts. I've had over 800,000 views on a single post and a million across two posts in one week.

Almost everyone in business who matters to you will be on LinkedIn. So make sure your profile is in best shape at all times. That includes:

- Use a professional or high quality photo, in formal or business-casual attire, and in a classy setting.

- Use keywords that relate to your business in your description, header, and title. This helps optimize your profile for search engines and get you organic views. For example, a marketer might use keywords like SEO, Growth, and Marketing Analytics sprinkled around her profile.

- If you're unemployed, always have something filled in for your current work, whether it's your own LLC or a project that you're a part of.

- Keep at least one to two previous jobs listed at all times.

- When explaining those jobs, use numbers where you can. There's no arguing with data. Percentages are usually your best friend here. For example, "Grew revenue 150% year over year," sounds a lot better than, "Grew revenue from $300 in 2017 to $450 in 2018." (Unless the dollar or growth figure is outrageously big for industry standards. Only then would it make more sense to use.)

- Ask friends for recommendations and to endorse your skills. If you're just starting out, have a few friends do it for you and you can do it for them in return.

- Add links to websites, previous projects, and media if you have any PowerPoints or videos that showcase your knowledge and expertise.

- Add connections. Do the best you can to surpass 500, so it shows 500+ as your connections number instead of an actual number. Join groups relevant to the job you're trying to get or the job you have. These are full of opportunities if you can get into active ones and start adding value.

- Add volunteer experience and any causes you support. It's always good to see people who give back and get a sense of some causes they care about.

- Use the publishing feature to syndicate written content you've created on other channels. It doesn't negatively affect your Google ranking for your original article, so it's worth adding to LinkedIn too. Use newsfeed posts to share the articles or create short form content that gets engagement. Comment and engage with others on the platform. It's a great way to get in front of executives and make your presence known.

Opportunities > Jobs

Exceptional people don't want just "good" jobs. They want great opportunities. So you have to ask yourself: are you good or exceptional?

The difference between a good job and a great opportunity is massive. A good job pays well, is stable and comfortable, and often clocks out at 5 p.m. A good employee will take a good job and work there for a decade, barely moving up the ranks, and get paid *maybe* 50% more than when they started, while learning nothing that will make them marketable to another job at another company. If they want to switch jobs, they're often forced to go backwards in their career in order to make a move.

An exceptional opportunity is one in which you know you're going to need to learn a ton, and fast. Where your colleagues will push you to be better everyday. Where your assignments and projects are heavily reliant on you, and you show the difference you make in the company day in and day out. You often leave the office after 8 p.m., but with a feeling of accomplishment. You take that job because you know it will lead you toward a much greater, more successful future.

In short, exceptional opportunities lead to exceptional careers. Don't be good. Be exceptional!

LOOK FOR TRANSPARENCY

You may be wondering how it's possible to gather all the information you need to determine whether a company is right for you and whether an opening is exceptional or just good. After all, official corporate communications are designed to put the company's best foot forward, and Glassdoor reviews can only tell you so much.

The key is to look for transparency. If it's there, you'll see it in the company culture. Executives you meet will share with you both their successes and their challenges. They'll open up about what the company wants to do better and steps it's taking to get there. People who work for the company will feel comfortable sharing positives and negatives to give you a rounded picture.

This transparency includes a clear path for promotions. In considering a job, you should know what the next steps are to work your way up. Some organizations have designed promotion paths with clarity. For example, a salesperson may go from Junior Sales Development to Senior Sales Development to Junior Account Executive to Senior Account Executive over a typical trajectory of four years.

No matter what job function you're in, understand what pathways are available to you. Maybe, in order to work at your dream company, you need to start in Customer Support. That can be a great opportunity, even if your dream position is in Marketing, because there's a path for you in that direction. It's important to know whom to work through internally in order to get certain opportunities and what performance metrics the company needs to see from you. Take, for example, a Customer Support Rep who spends her lunch break writing up marketing notes to present to the Marketing team based on what she's been learning from speaking to customers. Those are incredibly important interactions to a marketing team and important pathway building for an enterprising employee.

If a company can show you that kind of path for any position you're considering, it's likely a good business to work for. This is something you should always ask about. I recommend saying something like, "If I accepted this position, what would the next three to five years look like? What could be a potential path or a few potential paths for me?" Similarly, ask about how your take-home pay can be expected to increase. Working in sales, I've asked, "What is quota, and how many reps hit it last quarter?" This will demonstrate what you're likely to make. As a CEO, I like when candidates ask these kinds of questions.

Keep Your Options Open

Another thing I like as a CEO is seeing candidates come from different fields and show enough knowledge and interest to make jumping over to my company a legitimate possibility.

Millennials, in particular, like to move around, and today's businesses should adapt to—not resist—how we do things. Gallup found that 21% of millennials say they've changed jobs in the past year, more than three times the number of non-millennials who did so. We're also more likely to be open to new and different possibilities. Unless you have a family business, just about everyone is in the same boat.

Today's successful organizations need to adapt to—not resist—the way we do things, particularly since millennials are now the biggest generation in the workforce.

You should give yourself the same chance to experiment and adapt. Were you a marketing major in college? You don't have to work only marketing jobs. Did you study to become a CPA? That doesn't mean you can have only one type of job forever. Don't pigeonhole yourself. If you don't like it, taking a job in the field would just be throwing away time and money. The education you got in college can apply to other fields as well. Chase what you're passionate about now, and don't be afraid to take an opportunity that opens up.

Inside an organization, the same thing is true. Just because you're an entry-level sales development rep now doesn't mean you need to become an SDR Manager or Sales Executive next. You can go into customer success or product roles, or all sorts of other avenues if you take the time to learn the skills needed. Get to know other members of your company. Go to lunch with them and inquire about what their jobs are like.

Your twenties are the petri dish of your career. Let yourself grow and change.

THE TRUTH ABOUT
PAY AND BENEFITS

None of this means your pay and benefits are irrelevant. They do, of course, matter. When considering an offer, be sure to think long term.

For starters, this means not getting seduced by promises of equity in a company.

Equity is often bullshit. Yes, there are stories of people who got in early at Apple and Facebook and ended up rich for it. But in most cases, your startup won't be acquired for a massive sum, if at all. And the tiny percentage you get won't make up for years of hard work when you could have been making more somewhere else.

So while equity is nice, unless you're a founder and have a seat at the table, avoid getting hung up on it. If you're starting out and you're just another employee, don't expect this to be the venture that makes you rich.

There's also a big downside to companies that are too focused on equity. The big investors and shareholders can become obsessed with how the share price is doing, because they want to make short-term financial decisions for themselves, while losing sight of the big picture. So they might not care whether the product has great new features or if a conference went well. For your purposes, focus on learning and building the long-term success of the company as best you can. The more successful the company is, the more doors will open to you in the future.

So how much should you make along the way? When it comes to salary, you need enough to get by. But don't expect your salary to make you wealthy. I've found that people don't develop wealth through salaries. As AngelList founder Naval Ravikant says, "You're never going to get rich renting out your time."

Wealth comes in chunks—when a large chunk of assets liquidate. So in the future (which I'll address in this book), when you're one of the top people at a company or found one yourself, you'll be on your way toward wealth.

This isn't to say that you can't pull together a good amount of money in the meantime. As you know from the stories of my youth, I've always been into saving. You can end up living comfortably this way. If you want real wealth, understand that it lies down the road if you play your cards right.

Another key element of compensation is vacation time. Again, you should go into the working world with a realistic understanding. Some companies now promise "unlimited vacation days." But that's often just a way to avoid doing what some other companies do: pay you for days you don't take when a specific amount is offered. As a *Forbes* column by ADPVoice explained, "Under traditional plans, employees accrue vacation time that they can cash out upon leaving the firm. But with unlimited plans, there is no accrual and therefore no deferred compensation to cash out."

"Unlimited" vacation time also backfires when employees feel nervous or insecure about being seen as taking too much. Not providing a definitive guideline makes employees think twice when planning a vacation, causing them to take less time than they normally would've. So don't be lured in by a promise of unlimited vacation time.

I also recommend against bringing up paid time off during your job interview. You can often find out a company's vacation policy online, and if the company makes you an offer, the information will be included there.

When it comes to using that time, my rules of thumb are that you make sure your work is done before you go off on vacation and set expectations with your team so you don't become a bottleneck. Give them a chance to bring anything to your attention in advance by writing an email like, "I'm going offline next week. Is there anything you can foresee needing while I'm gone? Anything I can do before I leave? I won't be able to be immediately responsive, so please advise by (provide a date), and I'll see what I can get done before my vacation."

Do take vacation. You absolutely need to rest and recharge. And it's good for business. "Employers are finding that the benefits of having employees take time off far outweigh the advantages of keeping them at the office," the Society for Human Resource Management reports. It adds, "Businesses that urge workers to take time off to relax, recuperate and recharge typically have lower health care, workers' compensation and turnover costs, and they benefit from higher productivity and employee engagement levels."

Even more striking is how much it benefits your career—nearly doubling your chance of getting a raise, according to a study by the organization Project: Time Off. "People who took fewer than 10 of their vacation days per year had a 34.6% likelihood of receiving a raise or bonus in a three-year period of time. People who took more than 10 of their vacation days had a 65.4% chance of receiving a raise or bonus," Shawn Achor and Michelle Gielan wrote in the *Harvard Business Review.*

When you're an employee, you have a right to take your time off when necessary. But when you found your own company, you won't have the luxury of taking much time off for a while. The ball will drop without you. Only when your team is hired out can you use much of your vacation time, and that can be years away.

If you've followed the steps I've laid out so far in this book, you'll be starting a new job and ready to give it your all. Now comes the next step: turning a job into a career path. You need to know the ropes of business in today's changing environment. As millennials, we can bring great skills and knowledge to the table. But there are also things we never learned in school. Learn these things now so you can hit the ground running at work.

How to Write and Speak Concisely

This is the most underrated skill and the number one thing any entry-level employee needs to learn. It's crazy that this still isn't taught in grade school or even college English courses.

We were taught how many cells are in a leaf, what igneous and metamorphic rocks look like, and how to dissect frogs. We learned all about sine, cosine, and tangents (remember "SohCahToa?"). But we're still not taught how to properly and optimally converse with other humans. That's freakin' ridiculous.

Learning this is especially important because the world has changed drastically from the days of writing letters with pen and paper and putting them in the mail. I remember when people outside of white-collar workers first began BBM'ing on their Blackberries and checking email on their phones. Since then, mobile has become a major player for eyeballs when opening, reading, and replying to emails.

That means, for you, there's a good chance this is the native way of doing business. And 90% of the time you spend writing, you're writing for email and messaging. You probably do at least half of that from a mobile phone, and the recipients are often reading your messages from their mobile devices. So, for starters, you need to learn how to make your messages short and to the point. That's not as easy as it sounds.

Do you remember your high school English class assignments? Your teacher probably instructed you to write 5,000-word essays. Then he graded it, maybe asked you to fix things or write a new 5,000-word draft. That was it, end of the assignment. It's a fine idea for a creative-writing elective. And I think it has its place in the curriculum at an earlier point, like middle school. But then it's time to learn to cut things down and think in a structured manner. That's much more practical for the real world.

There's a famous quote: "Sorry this letter is so long, I did not have time to make it shorter." (It's been attributed to the French philosopher Blaise Pascal, though also to others.) The point is, making a powerful point in just a few words can be a tough task. And these days, brevity in work messaging gets you farther. That's the skill you need: to be great at writing and editing something the recipient will actually want to read.

With this in mind, I've created the assignment that should be used in all high school English classes:

Teacher: "Write a 5,000 word essay on X." Student hands in the assignment. Teacher grades it and hands it back.

Teacher: "Now take the graded essay and make it 500 words without losing any of the main message." Student hands in the assignment. Teacher grades it and hands it back.

Teacher: "Now take the graded essay and make it 50 words without losing any of the main message."

This assignment allows schools to teach students how to write creatively, while also teaching them how to edit and think in a more structured manner. To really think through what's important and how to pack a punch with fewer words. With this kind of assignment, we could be teaching our youth how to write, and then how to write practically, so we prepare kids for future jobs.

You can learn this now. Here are 10 tips to make emails more concise:

1. Write an email. Before sending it, go back and edit it three times.

2. Remove words that don't mean anything. Words like "really," "currently," "actually," and "very" are often filler words that just make sentences longer.

3. Only hit the spacebar once after a period, not twice. Cleaner, shorter, much better for email or text.

4. Enter is your friend. I was taught five sentences to a paragraph in grade school. That is not the case in email. Remember that on mobile, long paragraphs look like a screen full of endless letters and are immediately tiring.

5. Bullet point stuff if it looks too wordy all clumped together.

6. Dumb it down. People don't want to process what words mean. You want them focused on what you're saying, not how you're saying it. For example, write "use," not "utilize." There's a reason the top songs on the Billboard 100 are written on a third-grade reading level.

7. Write like you speak. Then go back and edit to make it more formal if necessary for a specific recipient.

8. Make calls to action (CTAs) clear. The action item usually deserves its own sentence. An example of an email CTA could be, "Do you have 15 minutes for a call on Wednesday at 2 p.m. PT?"

9. Never send a business email with emotion. If you're feeling emotional about an issue, cool off first. Then write the message and leave it for an hour. Come back to it and see how you feel before you send. If you have to question it, it's almost always a better idea to hit delete and come back later.

10. The only acceptable email styling is simple. I use a sans-serif font, black color, normal size. This is not the place to show your pizazz.

A good way to practice all this is to start blogging. How will this help you write better emails? My friend Scott Britton, named one of *Forbes'* 30 Under 30 in enterprise technology, offers this advice: "Creating content in a public setting forced me to get good at writing, as well as copywriting, which is incredibly important for modern sales and marketing professionals." I couldn't agree more.

Posting updates on LinkedIn is also helpful, because it limits characters. Start practicing this ASAP.

There's also a structure to a good business email. Keep this order in mind:

- Start with salutations.

- Ego stroke. Nothing over the top, just something simple like, "Really enjoyed your recent article on XYZ in *Inc.*" Or, "Congratulations on your recent round of funding."

- Introduce yourself.

- Now, the centerpiece of your note, you present an idea or question. In doing so, show that you understand the recipient's situation:
    - Appeal to his or her "pain point" (which *Macmillan Dictionary* defines as "a problem or need a business or company aims to solve").
    - Try a version of "Feel, Felt, Found," a technique in which you empathize with how someone feels, tell them about someone else who felt that way, and then explain how the other person found what you're offering can be a solution.

- Include an action item.

- Sign off.

We'll get more into the pitch process later in this book.

When you're responding to an email, I recommend you draft a note rather than clicking on one of the auto-generated options some programs offer you. At this stage, it's still pretty easy for recipients to see through that and realize you didn't take the time to respond personally.

Email Signature and
Out-of-Office Messages

Your email signature and out-of-office reply can also go a long way toward establishing a sense of professionalism.

As I explain in my book, *Hacking Sales*, too many people throw a bunch of images in their email signatures. I don't care if it looks pretty, don't do it. Make your signature as simple as possible. The only thing you should add is a link to recent positive PR. And if the headline of the story isn't that good, change it in the link.

Here's an example of a good signature:

[Name] | [Twitter Handle]
[Title] [Company name]
[Mobile/Skype] | [Office/Skype]
Forbes Names [Company Name] Top 10
Fastest Growing of the Year. Find Out Why!

Scott Britton updates his signature frequently to link to his most recent blog post. He measured the results and found that the 20 seconds it takes to update a signature link leads to more than 100 page views.

I recommend doing something similar with your out-of-office message. Instead of a generic note, try something like this:

"I'm currently traveling, with limited access to the Internet, and will be back [date].

In the meantime, check out our most recent article [company blog post, personal blog post, or recent good press].

If it's urgent, please contact [co-worker's name]."

This way, you're not wasting the chance to get eyeballs, even when you're offline. Just make sure it's professional. I like to straddle the line between, "I have a personality and my company culture is fun," and, "I work with Fortune 500 clients, so I need to keep this in line with those communication standards."

OUTREACH STRATEGY

Crafting proper emails is just part of a larger challenge: learning the art of outreach. In today's changing business environment, for our generation, there are all sorts of questions to navigate. Whom should you reach out to and how? Whom should you avoid? As you build your career, you'll need to ask people for stuff. You'll also have to make it worth their while to help you and be there for them when they need things. It's all part of conversational intelligence.

Here are my rules for business-related outreach. You can use this for job searches, sales processes, and anything in between.

If you're asking for something, don't focus on what you want. Focus on what the person you're reaching out to wants. For example, if you're looking for a new job, ask people if they know any companies looking for a kickass (job function/title). If they do know any, they'd be doing the company a favor as well by setting up an introduction. It can help build the relationship between the person you're reaching out to and the company where you might eventually work. Think how that might benefit everyone involved. Too many people simply ask for things, with no thought given to what others want or need.

The "friend zone" is bad in dating (in my experience), but great in sales and other business partnerships. If someone can help you and you think you can help them, do what you can to get in the friend zone as fast as possible. This means connecting with them as an individual first, not as an employee or company. Research on social, especially Twitter and LinkedIn, to find connections. Then get to know people before you ask for anything. If you're open to making friends, whether or not they can help you down the road, then there's nothing dishonest about this.

Before messaging someone on LinkedIn, find out what name they like to go by. Some people use nicknames or middle names as first names. Look at the recommendations and comments in their posts to see what their colleagues call them. I've found that when you take the few extra seconds to do this, your response rates improve significantly.

Want to get on calls with people you've never met? Remember that asking for their time is like asking them to give you money. So think about time like you think about a bank account. To me, time is worth more than money because it's finite. I can't get it back, create, or buy more. Every unproductive minute is one that I could've used to make money, work on myself, or hang with friends and family. So when someone asks me for a call, they're asking me to spend 30 minutes with them. Honestly, they'd have a better shot at asking me for $30.

Asking for someone else's time is hard. If you start to think about time as money, you'll have far greater success. You'll be more organized, more productive, and learn to understand how relationships work in the long term. Most importantly, you'll aim to provide tangible value up front, which is key.

Work to build trust. As a rule, people want to trust you. Get connected to them through a mutual contact. If you can't, at least make sure your online profiles are so good and clear that they see you as legitimate, capable, and honest. In sales terms, this would be your social proof or a referral.

In exchange for someone's time, try to offer some value for free. Maybe you can offer a free trial of something, a taste test, or even just a chance to tell you about a challenge they're facing so you can determine whether your solution works for them.

When it comes to your ask, clearly articulate how you can help someone, how long it will take, and how much it will cost. Be upfront about all of this. The more honest you are, the better shot you have of communicating why you genuinely believe it may be worth their time.

Sometimes you'll be the one receiving someone else's outreach efforts. If they ask you to set up an introduction for them, always check with the other person first. The only exception is if it's painfully obvious that both will love each other—for example, sending someone a high-value customer. And remember this rule of thumb: After someone does an introduction, the person who asked for that introduction should be the one who responds first.

Listen More

Learning all this will help you develop as a professional, no matter what field you go into. In every business today, communication is key. With time, you'll develop the right style that works for you.

But communication isn't all—or even mostly—about what you say or the information you provide. It's more about listening. You should be aiming for a 2:1 listen-to-talk ratio. As Richard Branson says, "Being a good listener is absolutely critical to being a good leader; you have to listen to the people who are on the front line." And Microsoft CEO Satya Nadella wrote in his book *Hit Refresh*, "Listening was the most important thing I accomplished each day because it would build the foundation of my leadership for years to come."

When you're having a conversation, wait until the other person stops talking before you respond. Ask questions to show that you're listening and following what the other person is saying. Remember this adage: "The person who asks the questions controls the conversation." Feel empowered to ask things. The more clear and concise your question, the better answer you will get and the smoother the conversation will go.

If you're ever unsure what to ask next, just repeat the last thing they said, but present it as a question. That's an invitation for them to say more.

If you end a conversation and feel that you did all the talking, you were not in control. You also didn't learn enough about the other person to build a business relationship. The more you know and understand, the better job you can do of ensuring that your solution really can help them. Like the Chinese proverb says, "He who asks a question is a fool for five minutes. He who does not ask a question remains a fool forever."

How to Tell a Persuasive Story

Storytelling is an incredibly powerful trait in life and in business. It can get people excited about something and help you sell or market anything—including yourself as you build your career. I've found two storytelling structures work particularly well for me, and I've given each my own spin.

The first is AIDA, which stands for Attention, Interest, Desire, Action. Here's what it means:

- **Attention:** The first step is also thought of as "awareness" or "attract." The idea is that you do something to grab people's focus. It could be shock factor, a powerful image, or personalization. A good example of this is an email subject line such as, "Why did you stop reading about our pricing, Brian?" Maybe the author of this email used an app to track users on their site and populate their data. If you received that email, it might stick out as a shocking thing that they knew your name and details about you, when you didn't think you gave them any information.

- **Interest:** What's going to keep the person reading or listening? One way is to be funny or entertaining. Another is to show how you're solving a problem they have. Once the reader opens the email, an interest grabber could be, "Would you like to know how we got your information and knew when you stopped reading?"

- **Desire:** Now that they're interested, take them to the next level. Bring them from, "hmm, OK that's cool," to, "ah, ok, I need that." Usually this is where you can take what interests them and layer on even more benefits, so what you're offering becomes even more attractive. Continuing with the email in the example, I might say, "What if we could provide you with the same technology to capture this data on your site? You would be able to follow up with users much faster, leading to more conversations with customers and, eventually, more revenue. Eighty-five percent of our customers see an uptick in interactions within the first month."

- **Action:** This is the call to action (CTA) we discussed earlier, in which you encourage them to take the next step. Always have a clear CTA. If your goal is to get them to take a meeting with you, you can say, "I'll be a few blocks away next Tuesday. Would you like to have lunch?" Or, "Here are some of my available slots to speak this week. Would you like to pick one?" In the case of our sales email above, you might close it with a link to signup or an offer to set up a call to tell them more and eventually close the deal.

The other storytelling structure I've found very useful is SCQA, which stands for Situation, Complication, Question, Answer.

- **Situation:** Start with the current state of affairs. This can be a look at an existing problem. For example, "I was walking to work yesterday when a rat ran over my foot. I looked up and saw more than 100 rats eating out of garbage bags that were ripped open. These bags were put out on the streets of New York City's Lower East Side neighborhood by restaurant owners waiting for city-organized garbage collection. This is a government-mandated process that the entire city abides by."

- **Complication:** What's the complexity behind the situation? Get people aware of it. "These rats are getting fed more than ever before, leading to a rapid increase in population. Studies by XYZ show the rats are carrying diseases from the trash that can spread to humans and potentially kill people if the problem is not stopped soon."

- **Question:** So what can we do about it? I.e., "So what can be done about this today, before people start losing their lives!?"

- **Answer:** Provide your solution—ideally, one that does not require people to make any big effort. "Simple. Garbage bags that have our special patented ABC coating are completely rat proof, therefore allowing restaurants to safely dispose of the trash. If every restaurant in the neighborhood used our bags, we'd see a dramatic decrease in the diseased rat population in only six months. When purchased in bulk, our bags are also five cents cheaper per bag than standard garbage bags, and they're biodegradable."

This is just an imaginary example. I don't really think rats are going to kill a chunk of the New York City population! But it's the structure that does the work in selling the service and making it easy to follow.

Check out the writings of David Ogilvy, known as "the father of advertising." Also *The Boron Letters* by Gary C. Halbert, who has been called "history's greatest copywriter." The more you read about great marketing, the more you will learn what makes people tick.

Another excellent way to get good at storytelling is to listen to TED talks (https://www.ted.com). Each presentation has a similar formula delivered in its own unique way, allowing viewers to tailor their story in a similar fashion. In one TED talk, I particularly enjoyed this quote from Dr. Brene Brown on telling stories in business: "Stories are just data with a soul."

I also recommend a *Business Insider* article on Pixar's "22 Rules for Telling a Great Story."

Learn Buyer Psychology

All this will help you learn about and interact with people. So will studying buyer psychology. As you spot opportunities and work your way up in your career, you're going to need people to "buy" what you're offering—yourself as an employee, your idea for the business, the reason you should get the promotion, etc. So take some time to dig into this.

You know what's a great source of wisdom on buyer psychology? Infomercials. I love watching good ones. Most infomercials have 30 minutes to wow buyers. Viewers can't ask questions, so they prepare with tons of market research to predict what the viewer is likely to think and want to hear next. Watching QVC or "As Seen On TV" commercials has taught me more about buyer behavior than any book or college class.

One of my favorites is a 28-minute Ronco video pushing his "Showtime Rotisserie & BBQ." It provides a perfect blueprint for things to hit on when creating any kind of marketing—whether a product pitch or a resume. In addition to following the SCQA storytelling method I discussed, it also includes:

1. **Social proof:** Great marketing includes third-party reviews from respected publications such as *Time* and *Forbes*. This infomercial has that, as well as professional chefs, heart doctors, chicken farmers, and even audience members of different ages, genders, and languages. It sends the message that experts recommend this. Apply this same idea to building your career by getting lots of recommendations and endorsements, and by getting colleagues to support you.

2. **Target buyer segments:** Buyers with similar profiles to target consumers are shown liking and appreciating the product. In the infomercial, you see a trendy dieter, hardcore foodie, coupon cutter, and busy parent. Words from someone who

comes across as being like you are powerful in influencing purchase decisions. In your career, get references from people who match all sorts of profiles, and share those with people in similar positions when you want something.

3. **Convenience**: To sell, always make clear that whatever you're offering is easy to use and saves time. (Remember, time is money, or even more precious than money.)

4. **Durability**: Whatever you've got, show that it's strong enough to last. In this infomercial we actually see someone using a hammer, ostensibly to try to break the device. In your career, it can mean showing that your idea for a business is proven to make a long-lasting impact.

5. **Broader good**: It helps sway people to show them that they would not only be saving money but also doing something for the broader good. This infomercial says that it leads you to use less power, so your electric bills drop and you can help save the Earth. In your career, show how hiring you, promoting you, or letting you run a project would lead not only to profits and cost savings, but also a chance to advance the company's values. (These are often in brand statements or corporate statements of purpose.)

6. **Style**: The infomercial makes the device look great and offers it in multiple colors to fit your kitchen. Whatever you're offering, always make it look its best. People respond to aesthetics. At Apple, Steve Jobs was obsessed with minute details of design. For you, this can mean "dressing for the job you want" or coming across in other ways—through social profiles and more—as fitting right in with the style of that job.

7. **Multiplying sales**: When the opportunity is ripe, expand your sale. This infomercial encourages you to buy one for yourself and buy more for friends. In your career, if you spot an opportunity, encourage your boss to give you even more projects, resources, or time for learning.

8. **Upsells**: You also expand your sale through offering higher levels or add-ons. Ronco pushes skewers and other implements to make the product even more useful. In your career, this principle could mean telling potential funders for your idea that if they invest more, they stand to gain more.

9. **Clever pricing models**: Rather than selling the product for $40, the company offers "two easy payments of $19.99." The use of multiple smaller payments helps convince people to buy. And, yes, all those nines instead of whole numbers help do the trick. They've been called "charm prices" using the "left-digit effect"—since we read the left-most digit first, people psychologically feel more comfortable with the purchase. In your career, this can mean, for example, starting at a lower salary with scheduled increases over time.

10. **Payment options**: Offering many ways to pay helps. The infomercial lets people use credit or pay straight from their bank accounts. As you build your career, particularly when you do freelance or consulting work, giving people many convenient ways to pay you can make a big difference.

11. **Guarantees**: Money-back guarantees can be a big help in selling. They, "evoke a positive emotional response, thereby increasing consumers' purchase intentions and willingness to pay a price premium," three researchers reported in the *Journal of Retailing*. Think about applying this to your own career by saying something like, "If I don't do a fantastic job for you, we can always part ways. But I will."

12. **Scarcity and urgency**: The infomercial drills in the idea that the deal being offered won't last long. How many times have you heard something like, "While supplies last," and, "You'd better act now!" These tactics work, with help from "FOMO"—the natural psychological fear of missing out. In your career, it can always be helpful to make clear that you have multiple opportunities, hear from headhunters, and are considering options.

13. **Memorable**: You want people to remember what you offered. The more you do that, the more likely they are to eventually buy. The Ronco infomercial, like most product advertisements, uses a tagline designed to stick in your head. This same idea applies to marketing yourself in your resume and interview. Hiring managers who remember you and think of you positively are more likely to hire you.

14. **Repetition**: Repeating key points can drive home a message and boost sales. There's a so-called "Law of Seven," suggesting that people need to hear something seven times before they take action. It's also known as "effective frequency." But it can lead to fatigue, making the consumer or hiring manager never want to hear about what you're offering ever again. So be careful not to overdo it.

15. **Clear call to action (CTA)**: "Call to order now!" The infomercial pushes you to buy now, with no meetings or next steps necessary.

They know their audience, and they've researched this sales process to a T. This is buyer psychology at its finest.

Small Acts Have Big Impacts

Small acts can also go a long way toward helping you build the kinds of relationships that will advance your career.

For example, have you ever received a gift or a compliment and thought, "Wow, I didn't realize how much I would appreciate this, but I do?" Back when my business partners and I were running a startup from Costa Rica (the one that built and ran social media presences for small businesses), our clients fell into a few distinct niches. One niche, the Ideal Customer Profile (ICP) was suburban, male/female, 40-50 year old, residential real estate agents.

After every close, we would send a $29 box of freshly baked cookies from the local bakery to the client at their office. When the cookies arrived, the other agents in the office would say things like, "Smells delicious! Who sent them?" They'd get our information. Not only did we make our client feel special, but it was a successful way for us to advertise to the rest of the office.

Two of my employees, a married couple, recently took a trip to Las Vegas for their anniversary. I sent a bottle of champagne to their room as a thank you. I've sent wedding gifts, baby gifts, donations to charities and kickstarters. Not even just for employees, but industry colleagues too.

I started doing these things because they felt good to do. Being called thoughtful makes me feel prouder than almost anything else. But I also came to see how helpful these small acts can be in the bigger picture, including for advancing a career. Every one of these acts builds relationships. And any one of those relationships could make a big difference in your career.

So ask yourself: what small act can I do today to have a big impact? From a simple thank you to a handwritten note to even remembering a special event or relevant information about someone, consider how you can become more thoughtful in your daily life. It'll pay big dividends in the long term.

CARRY A CHIP

On the flip side, don't listen to people who tell you never to "carry a chip on your shoulder." That chip can be a powerful motivator. It has been for me. Do carry one, just don't let it weigh you down.

I mentioned earlier that I still remember recruiters who passed on me. I also remember teachers who never believed in me. The drive to prove these people wrong has helped power me through challenging times in my career.

When I applied to Udemy, I had to do seven hours of interviews over two days. Then, when they didn't get back to me for a week, I followed up and still heard nothing. But I didn't give up hope. One reason was that I was so committed to proving the naysayers wrong. I was going to make it.

After I got hired, I used that same drive to succeed. When you're committed to proving yourself and disproving those who didn't believe in you, you can step into another gear that you didn't even know you had.

When my first book was published, my dad bought 30 copies. I asked who they were for. He said, "I'm sending them to your high school teachers and guidance counselor." Then he laughed, as if to say that it'll blow their minds. It felt great.

Trust Your Instincts

Sometimes you'll have a feeling that something just isn't going right. Don't ignore it. Trust it and look into it.

When I was working on the bike share business at ASU, we really needed to get a signature from a procurement specialist at the university to secure our partnership. Everything was going well, when suddenly our contact with the specialist went dark. I knew something was up. She wasn't picking up my calls or responding to my emails. I had a feeling the office was starting to look into other potential options. After all, we were just three 22 year olds, doing this for the first time at one of the largest colleges in the United States.

We had worked too hard on the business to let it be pulled out from under us. The university wasn't even thinking about having a bike-share program until we sold them on the idea. So in my mind, it was our right.

I went to the specialist's office one afternoon without an invitation and asked to see her. The assistant quickly dismissed me, saying she was in meetings all afternoon and that she'd get back to me. I said, "I'll wait, thanks." I sat there for almost four hours, patiently. I'm pretty sure my phone died (back then it definitely was not a smartphone).

When she came out, I got my answers. Just as I had suspected, the university was talking to bike vendors about other ways to create a bike-sharing program, leaving us out. She didn't fully understand the logistics of how we worked with these companies. We explained, and convinced her, that as part of our business we could help her office in selecting vendors to provide the bicycles that would be used within our program. She agreed, and we were invited to sit in the meetings.

Our plan was to contract with one of the providers anyway and manage the operations, so it was all the same to us. But had I not persisted, the university might have moved forward without us involved at all.

The Only Way to Truly Fail is to Stop

Many people will tell you not to be afraid of failure. I go one step further: support failure.

When people ask me to support their business or idea, I do it with one stipulation: If they fail, they have to let me back them again. Failure is often inevitable and is where the real learning is done. Your failures are just a page or two in the long novel of your career. If you learn your lessons, you're much more likely to succeed than someone who hasn't failed.

You learn the most when faced with adversity. Too many people run from this. Stand up and fight. Finish strong and sprint *through* the finish line, not *to* it.

You've probably noticed by now that I've learned to like wise, pithy sayings. They can help guide you when things get tough, and we all have tough moments. When it comes to failure, here are a few of my favorites:

> "The way through the challenge is to get still and ask yourself, 'What is the next right move?'…And not to be overwhelmed by it, because you know your life is bigger than that one moment. You know you're not defined by what somebody says is a failure for you because failure is just there to point you in a different direction." -Oprah Winfrey

> "It doesn't matter how many times you have failed, you only have to be right once." -Mark Cuban

Sara Blakely, creator of Spanx, says her father encouraged her and her brothers to fail, because it meant they were trying new things. She told CNBC that persistence is the key. "What you don't know can become your greatest asset if you'll let it and if you have the confidence to say, I'm going to do it anyway even though I haven't been taught or somebody hasn't shown me the way."

"It is impossible to live without failing at something, unless you live so cautiously that you might as well not have lived at all—in which case you fail by default." -J. K. ROWLING

"Pressure makes diamonds," a quote attributed to U.S. General George S. Patton, commander of the Third Army in World War II. It's a reminder that if something isn't stressful, it's probably not fruitful.

There are two more I like, though no one is sure where they originated. First, "You get what you tolerate." If something is awful, don't just complain or give up. Change it. And one of my favorites, "Success is not final and failure is not fatal. It's the courage to continue that counts." (It's usually attributed to Winston Churchill, but the International Churchill Society says he never actually said it.)

In my experience, the most successful people learn from failure, while the rest dwell on it or make excuses. They hang their heads, deflecting blame. They say, "The VCs didn't get what we're doing," or, "The competitors undercut us," or, "The market wasn't ready for it."

To grow, you must own your failures. The person who blamed the VCs failed to build the proper story or validate the business model. The person who blamed competitors failed to sell the value of the product. And the person who blamed the market failed to do the planning and diligence before starting the business.

In school, I failed classes. My bike-share effort failed. My business managing social media for companies didn't become the big success I wanted it to be. I've failed on plenty of initiatives as CEO of Sales Hacker. I've failed on investments and on trusting the right people. I've failed a lot. I've also had successes. And I've consistently found that failure makes you better than success does. It's much harder to learn from success, because your ego almost always gets in the way.

Job Hopping

Some people frown upon the idea of switching jobs every couple of years. But as I mentioned earlier, it's common practice for many millennials. (And *The Economist* notes that, for decades, younger workers have jumped around more than older workers.)

There are reasons switching jobs often can make especially good sense these days. The landscape has changed. More companies are popping up that need talent. And companies are growing so fast that a company may have needed an expert in something and then, suddenly, moved on to something else.

But I recommend that you try to stay in any business for at least a year if you want to display it on your resume. Anything less looks like you either made a bad choice taking the job or had a negative experience. That's OK, as long as you can clearly explain it and it isn't happening several times in just a few years.

The key is to pick jobs that offer you valuable learning experiences and to leave when you feel like you've finally hit the learning experience ceiling for that company.

When you're switching from one company to another that's in the same industry and about the same size, make sure you're going up a level or at least staying at the same level. If you're switching to a larger company, it's OK to take a step down in title. For example, being a VP at a 50-person company may be the equivalent of being a Director at a 5,000-person company. Focus on the level of responsibility the position entails.

If you're switching industries, it's a different story. In that case, you should make sure you take a job with an advanced title. That is your anchor or starting point in the new industry, and your previous experience won't make much difference to people in that industry—so make sure you start at the level you've earned from your experience. All other jobs you take from now on in this new industry will go up from there. For example, if you spent five years at Goldman Sachs in a sales or business development position, don't take anything less than a director role at a startup. This way your next startup job will be director or above.

WHEN IS IT TIME TO START MY OWN COMPANY?

I hope all the advice I've given you so far in this book helps on your journey to getting a job and delivering excellent work. But before we move on to Section II, let's address what may be the proverbial elephant in the room: the possibility that you may want to start your own company soon.

Start one only when the stars align. Those stars are the Five Ws:

1. **WHAT**: You've been toying with and workshopping an idea for months, and it won't leave you alone. It feels like your destiny. You've searched and haven't found another company doing exactly what you have in mind in exactly the same way.

2. **WHO**: Suddenly you can't help but notice that the right people, your potential collaborators, start to surface. Ones who could potentially help you. People with the right skills, experience, and passion for what you have in mind. People who could serve as a co-founder, a first customer, an industry advisor, or your entree into a community of like-minded individuals.

3. **WHY**: The reason you're excited about the idea is so strong that you can't help but talk about it to people as though it already exists. Your passion is contagious, and they begin to "get it." The more you talk about it, the more people try to poke holes in the idea. That helps you start to strengthen the concept with ideas that fill those holes or adapt to them. As you have these discussions, don't worry about people stealing your ideas. It's execution that matters. There were search engines before Google and social networks before Facebook. The ideas weren't

winners, the executions were. Sharing your ideas will help you properly articulate the problem you're looking to solve and will allow people to provide critical feedback.

4. **WHERE:** The good news on this is that, often, for a web-based business it really doesn't matter where you do this work from. I run my companies remotely. I'm a shareholder in companies spanning across the globe, and I know that you can do just as well in Warsaw as you would in San Francisco. But obviously, if you're looking to open a brick-and-mortar store or you want your team to work together in a shared space, you may need to make a move.

5. **WHEN:** You have the financial runway—an amount of time that you can afford to operate in the red—in order to take the leap. Or, even better, you have a few customers who are ready to buy and possibly even prepay before there's a product. With advancements in technology, pre-selling and product validation are more possible today than ever before. And, yes, fundraising sites like Kickstarter and Indiegogo can help. But be prepared for the possibility that your business will flop.

Many of the most successful startups got their results not just because of the idea, but because of timing. Take Uber for example. They needed customers to have smartphones. It wouldn't have worked years earlier with flip phones. When the market share of smartphones took off, Uber had all the ingredients put together to succeed.

Udemy, the online education marketplace I worked at, succeeded for similar reasons. Technology made it possible for anyone to teach a course online, since most people had high-quality recording hardware in their laptops and cell phones. Without this, our business could not have scaled properly. So strike when the time is right.

If you're not sure, then it's not the right time. Never start your own company just for the sake of starting a company.

Whether you're ready to advance your career path or strike out on your own—or a combination of both—you'll need the skills that help you to become a leader. That's next.

Section II

Becoming a Leader: Operating on the Job

If you follow the steps laid out in Section I, you'll be in a great job that matches your skills and your interests, starting off on your way toward a great career. Now, it's time to dig into some of the most important hacks to work your way up.

Learn to Initiate

Consider the fable of the farmer with two sons. Both are hard-working and efficient. When it comes time to retire and pass down the farm, the farmer passes the land to the younger brother. The older brother, upset, demands a reason why. Instead of answering, the father asks the older brother to go down to the farm of a man named Cibi and find out whether he has any cows for sale. The older brother comes back and says, "Yes, they have six cows for sale."

The father asks, "How much per cow?" The older brother returns to the farm, comes back home, and says, "It's $200 per cow." The father asks, "Can they deliver the cows tomorrow?" The older brother goes back to the farm and returns with a "yes."

The father then calls over to the younger brother, asking him to go down to Cibi's farm and find out whether he has any cows for sale. The younger brother returns and says, "Yes, they have cows for sale. Each one costs $200. If we buy six cows, they'll discount the total price by $100. If we wait until next week, they will also have special jersey cows. If we need them more urgently, they can deliver tomorrow." The father turns to the older brother and says, "That's why your younger brother is getting the farm."

The moral of this story is to always initiate. Don't just wait to be told what to do. Take control of a situation and see it through to the next step, going as far as you can before you have to return to higher-ups for further instructions. I've always been an initiator, and as a CEO I'm careful to hire only initiators. This way I know that, when I delegate things to my team, they'll come back complete.

Here's an example of how this can play out. If someone sends us a new tool to check out that could fix a tech issue we've been having, I send that to the appropriate person on my team. That person could respond with, "I checked out the tool. I think it should work for us." Or they can respond with, "I checked out the tool and spoke to a representative. I think it should work for us, as it integrates with our current technology stack, fits into our budget ($50 per year!), and solves our problem of only being able to export incomplete data. Now we'll be able to do XY, and in 3 months we should be able to do Z. Should I go ahead and set it up? I'm told it's quick and should only take 30 minutes."

Be that person. Make this a point in all of your interactions. Add value. Initiate.

Navigating Politics and Business Relationships: Play the Long Game

Too many people are shortsighted. It's the #1 career killer for those who aren't careful. I see it every day—from founders, executives, partners, employees, consultants, you name it. Everyone does it sometimes. I've been guilty of it too. But as I've advanced my career, I've become more cognizant and proactive. Now, I spot it everywhere.

Shortsightedness damages relationships. Your career is going to be long. Your community and industry are going to be small. With the help of the Internet, connections are more important now than ever before. Odds are good that I can contact someone you've worked with and reference check you in a few short minutes.

Over time, I've learned to see the worst ways people fail to see the big picture and damage their relationships and careers in the process. Here's how I counsel them to avoid these traps.

Don't Hold Grudges

Grudges are driven by ego. And they can prevent you from taking a great opportunity when it's offered. If someone contacts you with an ask, you might think, "This person did X to me years ago, so why should I do Y for them?" It's natural, but it only causes more problems. To succeed, judge each opportunity on its own merit. Maybe, when this person is asking you for something again, it will lead to good things for you. Just be sure to protect yourself from the downside this time to avoid letting them burn you again.

It boils down to looking forward. Consider the new opportunity and how it can play out for you in the long term. Don't focus on the past, just maybe be a little more defensive this time. In short, you should forgive (drop the grudge), but not forget (don't let them do it again).

Don't Burn Bridges

Even if you're dealing with someone who's unbearable, don't say anything you might regret. And don't air out dirty laundry about the person. The same thing goes if you're being let go from a job. As tempted as you may be, it's not worth talking badly about a company or manager.

It can be tough. It means being level-headed even when the other side isn't. For example, you may be in an argument over something in the workplace, like the strategic direction of the company. The other person may be basically kicking and screaming to have it his or her way. Take a different approach. Use facts and evidence to support your case in a professional manner. If they can't take that, then you might need to part ways with that person, severing whatever relationship you have. But I recommend salvaging what you can, even though it means swallowing some pride.

I've seen early stage company founders treat their executive level sales and marketing employees poorly, whether by not paying what's owed to them, bad mouthing them, or mishandling their exits—often through not giving them the proper time, courtesy, or sendoffs they deserve. Later, when VCs are considering funding the company, they reach out to those early stage executives and employees to get the inside scoop. When these folks describe what they went through, the VCs decide not to back the company.

I'm careful not to burn bridges, even when I have to fire people. *The Harvard Business Review* published a piece from me about this. I wrote, "Firing involves an element of selling. It requires empathy, asking the right questions, and guiding someone to your desired outcome in an authentic and honest way. While I'm selling people on the idea that they'll no longer be at the company, I'm helping them to see it's what is best for them as well. This may sound manipulative or callous; it isn't. When done right, it actually makes the transition easier."

Try your best to make sure the people you part ways with are champions for you and your company, not detractors. It'll go a long way—likely more than you'll ever find out.

Don't Voice Unneeded Opinions

When it comes to certain controversial topics, stay silent. If you're feeling tempted to weigh in, go do something else. Take a nap. Mow the lawn. Really, anything else is better.

Watching people jump into controversies is almost as cringeworthy as watching an episode of *Jersey Shore*. I've watched people time after time ruin their credibility with shortsighted LinkedIn and Facebook comments.

During the presidential election, I noticed countless people post on public channels. Not thought-provoking content, but moronic stuff like trashing all of the other candidates' supporters. Some of the folks making these posts were consultants or executives who should know better. They most definitely lost business from people who were offended. At the end of the day, the Internet is undefeated. What you say on it can be used against you at any point in the future.

However, if you feel so affected by something that you need to speak up on it, and you don't care who disagrees with you, then go for it. It can be opinionated and still be kept professional. Just keep in mind this piece of advice from my friend Jen Spencer, who heads up marketing for one of Hubspot's largest agencies: "Don't write anything online that you wouldn't say to your boss, client, employee, or mother."

Don't Talk Down to People at Lower Ranks

I've seen many workers start at the bottom of a company and go on to do amazing things. There are plenty of interns who become founders of very successful companies. You may be one of them. So showing disrespect to someone beneath you can only end up screwing you in the long run.

In fact, go the other way. Be attentive to those who could use your mentorship. The worst that can happen is you end up with a new friend. The best: your mentee starts the next company that Facebook buys for hundreds of millions of dollars, and maybe they offer you a nice little advisory stake to take home.

When I ran business development at Udemy, I didn't know what future direction I wanted to take in my career. So I contacted some other influential people who worked in business development, met up with them, and discussed their paths. Some were super nice and helpful. Some ignored me completely (which is fine). One guy agreed to a meeting, showed up late and half asleep, and just didn't really care. Why waste my time like that?

The people who mentored me are the first ones I think of now when new opportunities in business development come along. And that leads me to the next shortsighted thing people do.

Don't Forget Those Who Helped You

I've seen this far too often: Person A makes it big and forgets all about Person B who helped him get there. But you know what else I've seen happen? Person B makes it even bigger, and Person A's company burns cash. Or Person A gets fired. Now, Person A wants to rebuild a relationship with Person B.

Unless you're in the nine figures net worth club, you can't afford this. And either way, you can always come crashing back down. Keep up your relationships and really be there for people, especially when they need you. Don't just go seek them out when you need them.

Don't Nickel and Dime

Picture this scenario: you become a boss. An underling thinks you owe her a $500 bonus, and you think you can technically get away with saving the money from your budget instead.

The employee tells her friends what happened. One of those friends works at a business that you're applying to. Hearing this bad information about you, he advises against hiring you. You lose the opportunity—along with the pay hike it would have offered.

Short-term efforts to save a bit of cash lead to all kinds of bad scenarios like this. Screw over a partner, co-founder, or VC and get ready for pain when you need to raise money again. Screw over an employer and good luck getting hired in that industry again. Nickel and diming people does not pay off.

Don't Trash the Competition

People often get somewhat brainwashed when they begin working at a company. They start to think their company is the "good guy," and the competition is the "bad guy."

It's natural. You're financially connected to the success of your business, particularly when given equity (which, as I explained earlier, is often worthless). You know the people at your company and want them to succeed. And if you're at a startup, you buy into the idea that your company is the underdog, up against big corporations with lots of money.

As a result, some people start trashing the competition. Don't. First, it's bad business. Slamming your competitors makes you look more like a chump than a market-leading competitor.

But for your own career, think about the network. Your competitor has founders, executive teams, employees, and investors. These are all people who may feel you are burning them personally as you bash the results of their work—their business. That network effect keeps expanding as people from the competitor move to other companies and businesses get consolidated. When they hear your name at some point, they make clear they have no desire to work with you, and warn others against it. Being negative is a turn-off and can make you toxic.

Communicate

The good news is that most of these problems can be avoided when people communicate in a professional, productive manner. Sometimes, egos and pride prevent people from talking things out. Don't let that happen, as angst can carry on for a long time.

If there's a problem to discuss, go ahead and have a conversation about it, even if it's uncomfortable. Just don't let it linger.

And in your workplace relationships, care. If you do and they can feel it, you'll get ahead much faster.

Using Tact

This is one I'm constantly striving to get better at. Unspoken communication is hugely important. Often, your ability to hack your way to career success will hinge not on what you say, but on how you say it. You can say something really smart or really honest, but if you don't know how to say it with tact, you'll often look like a fool.

This may require practice. But it will never not be useful in business and personal relationships. Think of it as the difference between a message that reads, "I need this done now," and one that says, "Hey, could you please try to finish this quickly for me? We have a presentation today, and it would make a huge difference. Much appreciated!"

If you really feel you can't afford the few seconds of extra typing time, set up some keyboard shortcuts or enable dictation on your laptop. Trust me, your relationships will appreciate you for it. If you know how to not be a jerk, you should be OK.

NETWORKING

Now that you have a job, are you tempted to slow down your networking efforts? Don't. But do tweak them to make best use of your time.

Many people will vaguely tell you that you should be networking, that it's really important in your career. In reality, forced networking is rarely productive. Going to events and pinging people on LinkedIn, all for the sake of "knowing" more people, won't get you anywhere worth going.

For networking that is worthwhile, you need to have a direction. If you're currently working in one job but are thinking of moving into another field, go where people in that field are. If you're thinking of going out on your own and becoming a founder, go where founders and VCs go. Get more strategic than ever.

Don't go to just any and all events in that space. Find the best ones. Ask people senior to you, colleagues, and friends. Find out where you should spend your time so you don't waste it.

Walk into each event with a clear purpose in mind and stick to it. Be friendly, open, and willing to meet anyone—all while staying aware of your goal. Ask questions and be genuinely interested in the answers. Don't ask for things from the people you meet. That's for later on. Open up to them about what you're looking to do without pitching and without endangering your current job. Connections will happen organically.

As you network, keep in mind that you don't want to be the smartest person in the room. If you are, then you're in the wrong room. You want to learn from people smarter than you about something. I try to be the second dumbest person in the room. But if I'm the dumbest, that's perfectly OK too.

Invest in relationships. If someone does you a favor or makes an introduction that yields a big reward like funding, customers, hires, etc., you'd better send them something nice. If you put the time and effort into building positive relationships, you may not even have to ask when you need something. When I launched my coffee alternative company SUTRA, I wrote a post about it on my public networks. Quite a few highly influential connections of mine asked, "What can I do to help?"

I also recommend creating a list of IMFs, which stands for impressive motherf*&#ers. These are people you've worked with, worked for, partnered with, been mentored by, provided services to, etc., whom you want to work with again. Then find the chance to do so when the time is right. This system has come in handy for me time and time again.

Building Your Brand

The idea that everyone should build their brand gets preached a lot and yelled from the rooftops. But when people try to do it, they're often inconsistent and then give up after just weeks or months.

If you want to build a successful brand, start by writing about your work. Share your unique process; findings along the way; or tactics, tips, and strategies you've put into place that might be helpful for others. It will highlight your uniqueness and ability to execute—and rarely will anyone be able to truly copy you.

Make a habit of sharing things that add value, whether they were created by you, your company, or someone else. Share your own processes, thoughts, and opinions on your industry. Ask for feedback and have open, honest conversations.

Use social networks, but pick one or two that you can really build on. If you prefer video and your audience is business professionals, do YouTube and LinkedIn. If you prefer photography and your audience is consumers, try Twitter and Instagram. It's hard to conquer and properly focus on more than two platforms at a time.

Gary Vaynerchuk, Casey Neistat, and Simon Sinek are a few of the best brand builders on a global level that I've seen. Individual niches have their own especially successful brand builders. In the tech space, I admire Jason Lemkin, Tomasz Tunguz, and Neil Patel. Corporate executives who focus on building a brand can make it work in their favor too. They get the best job offers before anyone else because they're the most well known.

But brand building is also about bringing people together. Be a person who does that. Create an invite-only meetup, like the ones I mentioned earlier that led to Sales Hacker. In selecting people for it, put real thought into who will add value. Get your company to sponsor it if it's supportive to their business. If not, find another company to sponsor it. If you're bringing together a group of potential new customers or hires, businesses should be more than willing to provide the space, as well as some food and beverages. If you can, go to a few events like this first, so you can see how it's done. Search Google and Meetup, and ask contacts. Then start yours.

Understand that building a brand takes time. The results won't come overnight. That's why you really need to like what you do.

The good news is that you don't need to wait until you're employed to engage in this process. If you know what you want to be doing and are having a problem getting a job in that field, start writing about your interests and being vocal about them anyway. Start a blog, vlog, podcast, app, or something else to get going. This can actually give you a head start, and may do more to help you find a job than anything else you've done.

Building Expertise

Brand-building can start off with your interests. But to grow a following, you need to become an expert, a go-to resource, and someone who is absolutely needed. When someone in your network gets asked a question in that area, you want them to immediately recommend reaching out to you.

My favorite part about being an expert is that it compounds. Having your knowledge recognized can give you greater, faster access to even more knowledge. For example, if I'm advising a company and need to know about the latest modelings for compensation in New York City, I can easily ask my contacts and get multiple, high-quality answers almost immediately. They've turned to me for knowledge on sales automation, founding a company, virtual assistants, startup life, or another topic I write about, so I can do the same to them. We tap into each other's reservoirs.

It's OK to be a jack of all trades, especially as an entrepreneur. But find a sliver of something that you can be a true leading expert on, and doors will open.

Get Really Good at Building Processes

Most of the successes I've had in my career have come when I worked really, really hard at first, then figured out ways to hire out, build a more efficient process, or automate what I could. That allowed me to switch focus and work on the next piece of the project, the business, or something else I could scale.

For example, at Udemy, I had to build out a repeatable sales process. I broke it up into stages, including:

- **List Building**: Figuring out who our ideal customer profile (ICP) was, where to find them, and how to get their contact info.

- **Outreach**: Outbound emailing at scale meant personalizing the email just enough and automating the rest.

- **Conversation**: Once we got a response to the email, setting up the next step in the sales process, which was to have a conversation and get them interested in creating a course.

- **Onboarding**: After they'd given a verbal indication that they were interested, we made sure they followed through and started actually uploading assets like videos and quizzes.

- **Course Created**: Course finished, approved by the team, and ready to sell.

When I first created this process, I had to do every piece of it myself. I had to figure out our ICP by looking up complimentary or competitor platforms and seeing what worked for them. We were focused on educational online courses in the tech sector, so I went on Amazon and looked up bestselling books offering tech instruction. These were ideal teachers for our platform. Then to find their email addresses, I built a process around Googling their names and areas of expertise and following the links through to a contact address.

I had to do every piece of the process above, perfect it, document it, and optimize it before I could pass it off to someone else. But once it was good enough to delegate, it would run smoothly without me, freeing me up to crank on a new process that needed figuring out.

For simple and redundant things like list building, I hand these processes off to a team of virtual assistants that I've built in the Philippines. If it's something more high level, it goes to an employee or contractor in the U.S. We're scrappy, and the talent abroad is definitely good enough to take on many of these types of tasks.

The key to growth in business is to figure something out yourself, scale it so it can take place in a bigger way, then become unnecessary to it. Once you're no longer needed for it to run, you've done your job.

Of course, the process you build has to be good for this to work. Automation is a magnifier. It can make a good process great, but a bad process terrible. Don't scale bad businesses that don't make money. Make sure what you're working towards can one day be profitable and self-sustaining. Always figure that out first.

We all have the same 24 hours in a day. Distinguish yourself by getting the most out of it. The more you're able to scale and automate things, the more time you have to advance your career. That requires being resourceful. As Tony Robbins says, "It's not the lack of resources, it's your lack of resourcefulness that stops you."

You can find more on how all this applies to sales in my book *Hacking Sales* (hackingsales.com).

Basic Spreadsheet & PowerPoint Etiquette

While we're discussing work processes, a quick note on etiquette for two kinds of documents you'll certainly use often.

When creating spreadsheets you share with teams for execution purposes, don't use the bright first row of colors when highlighting cells, rows, or columns. Use the second or third rows with the dull colors. They're the two rows directly underneath the bright row.

When creating a PowerPoint deck internally to display information for your team, the best format is one in which the title for each page is a layer of a story. So the title explains the page.

For example, instead of a slide titled "2017 Growth," with a chart underneath, title the slide "2017 Growth Trending Up 40% YoY" (Year over Year). This will make it much easier for your team to follow along and understand immediately what the chart shows.

Also, send out the deck the night before or a few hours before the presentation, so team members have a chance to skim it. This can get them up to speed enough for the meeting to be concise and not take up more time than needed.

Reputation is More Valuable Than Money

The pieces we've just discussed—networking, branding, building your expertise, and developing smart and scalable processes—add up to create your reputation. That's worth more than money, because it will work for you 24/7/365. It's also infinitely harder to earn back once lost.

Be someone people can trust. Challenge assumptions and catalog your findings. Keep networking, even as you build your reputation—because that's when you've earned the right to an incredible network.

As you build your reputation, leverage it to keep moving forward. Leverage your time, your network, and your successes. Be a source of good and keep giving. That will continue to build your reputation. The worst thing you can do is get a big head. Just realize that no matter how good your reputation is, it's never too good, and you can always lose it.

Prioritize Your Time

When people say they're too busy for something, it's really just another way of saying that something isn't a priority for them right now. That's either because they're focused elsewhere and don't want to be distracted, or you didn't give them a good enough reason to make something else a priority. It's always up to the person asking for the time to get people to say yes.

If you get rejected, don't take it personally. Politely accept it or politely try one more time to make your case, then politely accept the result. It's OK not to take no for an answer, as long as you're OK with potentially burning the bridge.

You should take note of your rejections for two reasons.

1. They can help you determine whether you're prioritizing your time properly. Are you reaching out to the wrong people? Are you spending too much time making all sorts of requests of people, with too little reward? If you can't convince people to make time for you, is what you're putting in front of them even worth making time for? Perhaps your project makes no sense, you're asking for too much money, or you just don't have your pitch fully ironed out.

2. Consider putting yourself in their shoes. If you were them, what could someone say that might sway you to say yes? Think about new ways of presenting and framing your ask.

Refer back to the previous section, Outreach Strategy, for more on this.

Hiring & Delegation

As you work your way up, you may soon face the challenge of being on the other side of the hiring process. Lots of millennials at startups weigh in on hiring decisions. So you'll need to know the basics of what to look for.

The most important hack in this respect is to hire the best people you can find. I'd rather take longer to hire the right person than bring on somebody quickly, no matter what the role is.

There's a great quote that goes, "Give me six hours to chop down a tree and I will spend the first four sharpening the axe." (It's been attributed to President Abraham Lincoln, but according to quoteinvestigator.com, he never said it.) The idea is that before you execute a task, you should prepare by having the absolute best tools ready. Hiring the sharpest minds is just as important, and the results compound. Not only will you trust your hires to take things off your plate, but they'll also be the kind of people who can contribute new ideas and expertise to enhance processes, doing things even better than you would have.

When I first started hiring, I was worried. I thought, "How the heck can I hire the best when all of these other companies can afford to pay so much more?" Over time, I learned you can always afford the best, even if you're going up against bigger and stronger companies. It's hard, but possible.

The key is to make your best case. Explain that they could go elsewhere and get paid more, but by working with you, they can have things they value more. Ask them, "What are the top three to five things that are most important for you in working at a new company?" In their answers, you may find that the bigger and stronger company doesn't really have the upper hand.

For example, some people put more value on having an impact on the end product, or they prefer autonomy and being trusted to get work done their way. Or they may prioritize feeling passionate for the product they're working on. Knowing these answers allows you to make your case and tailor it to the things they want to hear.

Also emphasize the long-term benefits of working with you instead—what they'll learn, what opportunities they'll have, whom they'll meet, etc. In short, tell potential hires the lessons of this book.

When a hire is made, you'll have to be willing to delegate work to them. As a bit of a control freak, I can find delegation scary. However, I knew that if I didn't learn to do it, I'd never be able to scale a business or manage a team.

Delegation often means taking one step backward and two steps forward. It may take the new person time to get up to speed, so there will be a loss at first. But it won't be long before you're pulling ahead as a result of the hire.

To delegate well, put your processes in writing, as clearly as possible, so someone else can pick them up quickly without requiring your time. Writing these can also help you smooth out each process, because it forces you to drill down to the problem that the process is meant to solve. (As American inventor Charles Kettering said, "A problem well stated is a problem half solved.") The writing process also helps you think through steps you take for granted, potentially showing you where the holes or hidden roadblocks may be.

Recently, I had an employee who was a terrific asset to the team, but had too much on his plate. I told him that if we couldn't lighten his load, he'd be a bottleneck to the organization. The problem was that he was reluctant to delegate tasks to others, afraid they wouldn't do a good job. So he and I worked together to fix that.

Delegating doesn't stop after you've handed off responsibility for a task. You have to keep updating and adjusting to see what works best. If you don't learn how to do all this, you'll never be able to grow your business or rise through the ranks at your company. You can't do it all yourself. There's no way around it.

Providing Negative Feedback

As you work your way up, you'll find that another tricky part of managing people is providing them with negative feedback when necessary.

In the past, I used a technique called the "Stop, Start, Continue" model for my employees. I found this to be moderately effective. I set an expectation that every time I had a one-on-one meeting, I would give the employee something to stop doing, start doing, and continue doing. Since they became conditioned to expect a stop and a start, they didn't feel shocked to be getting these bits of negative feedback.

But over time, I've switched to a refined version of the Compliment Sandwich. I start positive, finding something to praise. It allows people to feel heard, appreciated, or reassured. Unless the person is being fired, I want them to feel safe and know that no one is going anywhere.

Then comes the negative feedback. For this, it's super important to be well prepared. Your feedback should be specific, with ideas about how to do better. You should even rehearse it. Think through what their pushback or reaction might be before you speak to them, and prepare to address it. That way, you can be confident and strong in delivering constructive criticism, while still using tact.

For the end of the Compliment Sandwich, paint the picture of how incredible they, their life, or their work could be if they took the feedback and nailed the execution. Emphasize how you will support them as they work through that process. Maybe even remind them of things you're working on doing better, so you're in it together.

Providing negative feedback properly is important, because you want both sides to come out feeling motivated, not defeated, no matter what your desired outcome.

Building a Remote Culture

You may think of all these interactions as taking place in an office together. That's not necessary. I'm CEO of my company, Sales Hacker. As I write this, it's the end of a year in which I spent three months in San Francisco, three months in New York City, a month in Italy, a month in Bali, two months in the Hamptons, and two months on the road in all sorts of places, including the Maldives, Paris, Tokyo, Mexico, San Diego, Austin, Alaska (for the Northern Lights), Miami, Los Angeles, the Philippines, Wisconsin, Philadelphia, Salt Lake City, Las Vegas, and the Grand Canyon for a mix of work and play.

I thrive on it. But even better, my team is happy, works hard, and gets more done than most teams of a similar size and budget. They enjoy this same flexibility to work from wherever. It's a huge benefit that helps me attract great employees, building my businesses and my career.

To make a remote culture work for you, there are four central components to address:

- **Employees**: How you hire, manage, structure, and communicate with your team.

- **Your own work style**: Everyone works differently. In addition to giving your employees the flexibility to find how they tick, you need to do the same for yourself. Embrace your quirks while still setting a great example.

- **Other benefits**: Cost savings, competitive hiring, more time in the work day per employee. We'll get into it all.

- **Drawbacks**: Of course, it's not all sunshine and rainbows. There are drawbacks to working remotely.

Let's go through all of these, step by step.

EMPLOYEES

Hiring

Look for people who are self starters. This is true for any kind of work setup. The recruiting company ERE Media says hiring self-motivated people is, "the single smartest thing a hiring manager can do." And for remote employees, it can be especially crucial. In *The Harvard Business Review*, a man who spent a year working for WordPress explained how the company ran a 100% remote workforce. "If employees are self-motivated and empowered, remote work can accelerate productivity," he noted.

It can help to hire people who already have a track record of working remotely. In interviews, they can explain how they stay motivated and work as self-starters. I've never hired anyone that ended up failing due to remote work style.

It's also important to get past the idea that interviews always have to take place in person. Many of the people I've hired, I never met face to face before offering the position. Why would a face-to-face interview matter, if we don't work face to face?

Referrals are also key. We look for people who are somehow connected to our business. Sometimes you discover fantastic employees this way, serendipitously.

The younger generations are actually quite used to working remotely. Many of them were native to the first chat applications like AIM. So if you hire fellow millennials, Gen Z workers, or the following generations, expect this to feel natural to them.

Managing / Team Structure

Managing gets a bit harder when your team is remote. You don't know what people are doing or thinking as easily, and there aren't open door opportunities for them to share. So you need to be proactive in asking questions if you see activities dropping, such as fewer tasks done in your project management app, or engagement decline, such as decreased responsiveness on your communication app or email.

I don't make people work certain hours. But they do need to be available during operational hours. I say that U.S. employees should be online in their time zone from 9 a.m. to 6 p.m. That means they're reachable, so they don't become a bottleneck. For employees in other parts of the world, we determine work schedules based on what works for them and what tasks they're facing.

But being reachable doesn't mean being at your desk. I tell my staff that if they feel more comfortable going to the gym during the middle of the day and working early or late hours, that's fine by me. I don't care when your work gets done, I just care that it gets done. But if a colleague needs something from you at 1:30 p.m., get it to them in a reasonable time period so you don't slow down workflow.

Everyone is judged on work done, both quality and quantity, not hours worked. Because we're remote, the leash is shorter. If someone isn't getting their work done, we don't wait very long before addressing it, and if we have to, rectifying the situation by letting them go.

To help us all stay connected, we use collaborative tools such as Slack, Google Docs, Asana, Trello, HubSpot CRM, UberConference, and Gmail. New tools pop up all the time, and we adapt.

In any company, one of the key common characteristics of the most successful people is responsiveness. The best entrepreneurs, employees, and salespeople are all highly responsive. And because it's extremely helpful in a remote company, we set that as an expectation up front.

Full Time Employees, Contractors, and BPO

We have a good mix of full-time employees and contractors. Having some full-time employees is important because, if you get the right people, they'll tend to think of the business as if it's their own. But contractors are a great option because you can add and subtract easily by giving them more or less work based on the ebbs and flows of business throughout the year.

For example, when we're doing conferences, we have more work for a marketing contractor. But during other times of year, we cut back. Because we use contractors, we don't need to hire or fire to make these kinds of adjustments. You can't really do that with full-time employees.

We also use virtual assistants, which fall under the category of business process outsourcing (BPO). For more than six years, I've had a team of these workers in the Philippines. They do everything that a U.S.-based employee would do and speak perfect English. We give them a set of the more mundane, redundant, and time-consuming tasks, such as building or fixing email lists, uploading headshots to our conference web pages, and adding links into blog posts. They're an incredible asset that I've leveraged since my start in tech.

Virtual assistants are better than most U.S.-based employees that do similar functions, and they cost a fraction of what a hire in the U.S. does. But where they live, the amount of money I'm paying them goes a long way.

Personal Work Styles

How I Work

I work on hot and cold zones, and encourage you to do the same. I work when I'm feeling "in the zone," and take a break when I feel like I'm not fully there. Here's my typical work day if I'm on U.S. Pacific Time:

- Wake up in the morning around 7 a.m., do some stretches, and jump right online.

- Work from 7:15 a.m. straight through to 8:30 a.m.

- Take a break for an hour and go to the gym, take a spin class, or do yoga.

- Hop back online through 1 p.m. and eat lunch.
- Take another break if I can for an hour or two.
- Work through 6 p.m.

I get anywhere between five hours and twelve hours of work in every weekend. I also spend time with my girlfriend, go out to dinner, play pick up and rec league hockey, go out with friends, play with my dogs, travel a ton, and visit my nephews and other family. At this time of my life, I find there's plenty of time for all of it.

I also keep my work varied. Having different projects you like can be exciting. It's always good when you can have fun making money. So I find some time to work not just on Sales Hacker, but also on other projects like SUTRA. I write columns published in *Forbes*, *Money*, and *Inc.*, and I write articles and updates on LinkedIn.

My routine and flow change somewhat when I travel. This can be tricky, but I adjust. For example, when I'm in Sedona, I take advantage of the great trails and hike every day. So my routine gets broken up quite a bit. But I tweak it to make it work.

No matter where and when you're working, I highly recommend setting up a workstation for yourself. Keep it separated from other distractions. You need to make sure you have an "office."

If your significant other or friends are in the same house or apartment as you, make sure they know that when you're in your "office," they should only reach you by text. It may seem ridiculous at first, but it isn't. It's a great habit that will help ensure you concentrate and maximize the results of your work time. I keep Slack and iMessage up on my laptop. If my girlfriend needs me, she can shoot me a note on one of those, and I'll respond quickly by message without breaking my flow, or I'll wait until it's a good time to stop and leave the "office" to engage fully.

Other Benefits

Aside from the lifestyle benefits of having this kind of freedom, there's a long list of pragmatic, immediate business benefits to building a company entirely around a remote culture.

For starters, the lack of overhead saves a ton of money. In most cities, an office for a team our size could be anywhere between $3,000-10,000 every month. For that amount of money, I can hire another employee.

Employees skip the stress and hassles of commuting and get their time back. My VP of marketing would spend 90 minutes a day commuting if we required presence at an office in New York City. During that time, he's instead getting more work done—and fitting in a few games of basketball at the gym. He needs this time to practice if he's ever going to beat me! As I wrote in a *Money* column, "I know that stress destroys productivity. These days, many people aren't letting go of stress as much as they should, even when they get home. Playtime helps solve that and boosts innovation."

I can also hire people anywhere. My pool of potential candidates is as big as the world. And people are cheaper outside of most cities, especially San Francisco and New York. The costs of living in these cities is out of control, so salaries need to be in line with that. For what we're doing, talent is abundant elsewhere.

And everyone is incredibly loyal. We interact as a team every day online, meet up a few times a year at our conferences, and go out for fun team-building trips. We do weekly stand-up meetings over the phone or online, and a monthly call to align everyone and go over big wins.

Drawbacks

But as with anything, there are drawbacks. To make remote culture work, you have to prepare for and address these.

Less face-to-face time means the ball can drop easily without good processes. People may forget to check on a task in the management system, or two people may each think that the other one is handling something.

Working remotely can also crimp the great brainstorming and spontaneous developments that can come from being together. When I worked at Udemy, we would get beers at 5 p.m., hang, and talk about the business. Sparks would fly and good ideas would emerge, just from chatting and feeding off each other's energy. Now, running Sales Hacker as a remote business, I miss that.

But I've found that with a good culture and the right people, you can make something similar happen in different ways. We do lots of group chats and brainstorming at night. By fostering a culture of innovation, we can get great results connecting remotely.

Also, the best employees are the ones who come up with ideas and make things happen on their own, without the need for structured brainstorming. So you can have a lot of innovation even with less collaboration.

If you become a boss and your employees trust you and are happy, they'll move mountains for the company—regardless of whether they're in or out of an office.

Remote businesses can find it harder to build culture, but I haven't seen any loss in brand loyalty or employee engagement. In fact, having now worked for remote and non-remote startups, I'm a big believer in remote and may never go back to having a traditional office. Many people feel this way, which helps explain why it's quickly becoming a new norm. *The New York Times* reported that the percentage of people who work remotely four or five days a week jumped from 24% to 31% between 2012 and 2016.

When You're Better Off Renting Than Buying a Home

To make this kind of job hopping possible, you're probably better off renting, rather than buying your home for now. It's also usually the smarter move financially.

There's an old, outdated belief that owning your home is always the better financial decision. It's wrong, particularly in your 20s. As *Investopedia* notes, "There are tremendous financial benefits to renting as opposed to buying a house of your own."

When you calculate all the costs that go into homeownership and the way a mortgage can make it tougher to pick up and move when an opportunity comes along, you see that freedom and cost-savings often make renting the better choice. The way I see it, buying homes is for people who make salaries for their entire careers. But if you're thinking of ever becoming an entrepreneur and starting your own company, investing in your company is a better use of your money.

More and more people are figuring this out. Fewer people are buying houses and more are renting. Homeownership among people younger than 35 has dropped more than 18% since 2006, *Time* reports.

Side Projects

I'm a big believer that you should also have an alternate passion project at any given time. Not multiple projects, but one that really excites you. It allows you to flex a different muscle than you may normally stretch during your day job. It gives you a release, while also training you in unique skill sets that can benefit your career.

However, there are times not to do this. Do not have a side project if are in the middle of getting a company off the ground. That needs and deserves your full focus. Also, if you're still cutting your teeth at a new job and the side project could take you away from your day-to-day responsibilities, put it off. Early in your career, you will benefit most from making sure you crush your job. You'll know when you're established enough that you can afford to spend time on a side project.

My VP of Marketing, for example, cut his teeth and earned my trust. He now has a side project helping musicians market their music. It merges his two true passions, music and SEO. I love it, because he learns things that he can use when working for Sales Hacker, like SEO tricks and new Wordpress plugins.

It's also always good to see your employees put real effort and work into things they care about. As an employer, I'd much rather have him honing his skills doing what he loves than watching the latest episode of some hot new TV show.

Section III

PERSONAL DEVELOPMENT

In 2017, I had an emergency appendectomy just 48 hours before our industry's largest conference was about to begin. It was terrible timing, to say the least. Despite some pushback from my nurses, I was out of the emergency room and on my way home only two hours after the surgery. We had work to do, and we needed to execute.

I trusted my team, but this was a big event, and I needed to be there in full force. I had two days to recover from a surgery that takes most people two weeks. Once the event started, it was four days straight of standing, walking, talking, and entertaining conference attendees, our potential partners.

I was pushing my body to the extreme, and it was doing just well enough to get by. Right after the conference, we had planned a trip to the Grand Canyon. I wasn't going to reschedule that, as it was hard to find the time to get there, so we did it. So in one week, I underwent surgery to remove a ruptured appendix, organized a four-day event inside of a 300,000 person conference, and hiked along the South Rim of the Grand Canyon. I thought I was Hercules, but I was just a hard-headed fool. After the Grand Canyon, I crashed both mentally and physically. I had pushed myself beyond reasonable limits, and the limits pushed back.

Everything is aligned. Your mind and your body work in tandem, so if you don't take care of one, the other will surely crap out on you in due time. Out of serendipity, I saw a quote around this time that really stuck with me. It said, "You can't pour from an empty cup. Take care of yourself first."

Career Hacking isn't going to get you very far unless you're properly taking care of your mind and body. It's a big part of developing into who you are and who you strive to be. Don't get so lost in work that you forget about life and the engines that make you run both short and long term. Making sure you develop as a person will benefit your career in tremendous ways.

Don't Let Others Dictate How You Feel

When I was right out of college, I was stuck in some bad habits. One of the worst, which is very common, is that I kept comparing myself to others—people I grew up with, worked with, or my parents and friends spoke about. It's a natural thing to do. Since I'm a competitive person, it was particularly acute for me.

It took me a long time to realize that this is a lose-lose situation. For one thing, I never really knew how other people were doing. What looks good on the outside isn't always so. I've seen people raise a ton of money and live lavish lifestyles, only to have it all suddenly go belly up. And there's always going to be someone doing better. Even if you're Mark Zuckerberg, guess what, there are still a few people richer than he is. You think he worries about that? I doubt it.

The only thing you can really do is just do *you*. Do it better every year. It's a goal that's both quantifiable and controllable.

As part of my excessive comparing, I also felt a lot of social pressure. Like I had to be married soon or buy a house by a certain age. That kind of pressure is like a weight. It ends up crippling you if you let it. So learn not to cave to it. If you're single and your friends are all settling down, just be happy for them and for yourself for making your own choices. (I also believe that everyone still alive in 2050 is probably going to be able to live forever, thanks to modern technology. So what's the rush? It's not a crazy idea. Several researchers say there "may be no limit to how long humans can live," *Live Science* reports.)

There may be times that you look around and think that "everyone else" knows what they're doing with their lives but you don't. The truth is nobody knows what they're doing. Everyone is lost. Don't be fooled. You're normal.

Meditation

As a hyperactive, extremely competitive person, learning how to meditate was one of the most frustrating things I've ever done. There is this common misconception that meditating means shutting off your brain and transcending into a state of nothingness. That's not meditation.

Meditation, to me, is simply the act of pausing, recognizing your thoughts, and learning how to manage them. If you can do this well, it provides you with the ability to manage your relationship with yourself and your relationships with others on a whole new level.

Meditation is definitely a skill and, like any skill, needs significant time and practice to master. When I first started learning, I was forcing it. I wanted the ability to empty my mind to come and come quick. I would exit my meditations and be more agitated than when I started, because I was frustrated that I couldn't pick it up.

Then I realized that I was missing the point. That common misconception is why the thought of meditation is more intimidating than actually meditating. In fact, had I spent more time actually practicing meditation instead of trying to learn how to do it, I'd probably be a lot better at it by now! But like many other sections in this book, my pain is your gain.

It took a long time, I spent a lot of money, and I tried some pretty extreme methods, but here's the practice I do daily that finally works for me.

I find a quiet or semi-quiet place where I can sit with my back against something. It can be on a chair that has a back, against a wall, or on the floor against the bed as long as I have back support.

If I'm in a chair, my feet are flat on the floor. If I'm on the floor or a flat surface, I sit with my butt on a pillow and my legs folded in front of me off the pillow. You want your knees to be lower than your hips to protect your back from straining. I put my hands on my knees, palms down, because that's comfortable for me. Do whatever is comfortable. You can do this in any clothing, but the more comfortable the better.

I like to do it first thing in the morning, but any time of day works. I aim for 12 minutes, once per day. But even just a minute a day can help.

You see, I'm building a big case for no excuses here. You can do it in any room, with any level of noise, with any attire, any time of day, for any amount of time. It's true. Obviously optimizing your surroundings for your session helps, but it all works.

In my ideal session, I shoot for 12 minutes. The first minute is for settling into calmness. I'm in my seated position, with my eyes closed and hands palm down on my knees. I start to relax and pay attention to my breath. Breathe in, breathe out. Just letting the dust settle in my mind.

After the first minute, I go into my meditation for 10 minutes. Breathe in, breathe out. Focus on the breath. When you breathe in, let the voice in your head say "in." When you breathe out, let the voice in your head say "out." No need to try and alter your normal breathing rate. Just breathe calmly and deeply, so you feel yourself filling with air.

Once I have this repetition going, I like to imagine that I'm sitting on a beach right in front of where the waves would break and wash up to my feet as I stare at the ocean. It's a sunny day, the sand is powdery and white, and the water is crystal clear. When I'm breathing in, a wave is slowly drawing back into the ocean. When I breathe out, the wave gently tumbles and washes up to my feet. I'm paying attention to the breath beginning and ending, using the visual of the wave.

When a thought interrupts you, which it definitely will and is totally normal, recognize it, spot it, and call it out. Then reset yourself and go again. In. Out. In. Out.

The last minute is for coming out of the meditation. Sometimes I need a little longer than a minute, but this is the time where you bring yourself back to reality. I keep my eyes closed for this last minute, start to congratulate myself on a good session internally, and then let my mind go back to wandering normally before opening my eyes.

The key to meditating consistently is to keep it friendly and realize it will take time to master. Getting through each session is progress. That's why it's good to pat yourself on the back.

I've found it very helpful to use a good interval timer. I use Meditation Timer - Simple Insight and Zen Timer, a free app on my iPhone that offers a mellow alert for each interval of my meditation. A bell goes off after the first minute, signifying the end of prep time. After the eleventh minute, another bell signifies the end of the ten minute meditation. Then after the twelfth minute, a longer bell with a ring signifies the conclusion of the session. This way I don't need to check the time and can be fully present in the routine.

I previously tried Transcendental Meditation. I have friends who swear by it and say it changed their lives, but I couldn't get into it.

I sometimes meditate at a yoga center in San Francisco, with a swami who uses a mantra. And sometimes I practice with my mother, who likes to use a countdown method.

A few years ago, I did a three-day OSHO Dynamic Meditation retreat. We spent hours jumping around, punching at air, and breathing in and out as fast and aggressively as possible. Then, while mentally and physically exhausted, we lay flat on the floor in a traditional meditation that includes paying attention to breath, while embracing your feelings and the noises around you. It was the deepest meditation I've done, but not something I could reasonably do daily.

No matter what your style is, meditation is worth investing time into as soon as you possibly can. Just know that it'll take a while to figure out what works for you, and don't to get too hung up on it if it doesn't click right away.

Organized Journaling

As a business owner with obsessive-compulsive disorder (OCD), I've often faced anxiety, wondering whether I can or should be doing better. And I sometimes get far too obsessed with the destination I want my business to arrive at, rather than the journey of getting there.

I found a way to beat this through a technique that has changed me as a person, a professional, and an entrepreneur: journaling. It goes a long way toward helping you compartmentalize what you're dealing with and remain ambitious while still enjoying the day to day.

Every Monday morning, I write a list comprised of four parts:

1. Things I'm grateful for. I list everything and don't hold back. If you do this, you'll often discover that there's a lot more than you thought. And it feels awesome to start the week with an attitude of gratitude! Thinking about this daily can also be helpful during stressful times, even if you just give it some thought while staring at the ceiling the moment you wake up.

2. Things I'm stressed about. List things that are sticking out in your mind that you can or cannot fix. You'll find there's less than you thought and that much of it actually is fixable. Identifying these things is the first step to coping with them. Writing them down also helps to remove the emotion from them, making them easier to accept and start trying to solve.

3. Ways in which I grew last week. List even the small ones. It's always good to recap incremental growth so that you recognize it's happening. It's amazing how much you grow day to day and don't realize until you shine a light on it.

4. This week's to-do list. After these other elements are laid out, visualize your attack plan for the week. I keep mine in Google Docs, but a classic pen-and-paper system can work just as well. Do it however you like, as long as you can access it on demand.

If you want to go a step further, you can even break each section of your journal into macro (long-term) and micro (short-term) goals. For example, if I'm stressed about a long-term business goal, like pulling off an event in a few months, that's a macro item. If I'm stressed about a call this week that I need to have with a vendor for that event, that's a micro goal. Seeing it broken out allows me to understand how I can compartmentalize my problems and prioritize my to-do list.

Schedule five or ten minutes for this every Monday morning. You'll thank me.

Yearly Goal Planning Guide

At the end of every year, I put together a goal planning one-pager based on Warren Buffett's famous 25-5 Rule. He says to write down up to 25 goals you want to accomplish (e.g., learn to speak Spanish fluently). Then circle your top five goals. Next, go ahead and delete or cross out all of the other goals, because that's all you really have the bandwidth to focus on for now. Knowing you won't have time to do all of those things makes it a lot easier to focus on the five you feel you *must* accomplish.

The difference between my exercise and Buffet's is that I use a 5x3 approach. I have five goal categories and three sub-goals tied to the larger goal. It has worked extremely well for keeping me on my desired track. The categories are:

- **Financial**: Are there investments you want to make, companies you want to start, deals you want to close?

- **Physical**: This could be fixing your posture, going on a diet, losing a certain amount of body fat, gaining a specific amount of muscle, etc.

- **Mental/Emotional**: Perhaps you want to start seeing a therapist regularly, learn to meditate, or spend more time with friends and family.

- **Personal Growth**: Want to read for 15 minutes or listen to a podcast on the way to work every day?

- **Help**: You may want to donate a certain amount to a charity, spend a number of hours volunteering, or perhaps help millennials with their careers. (See what I did there?) More on this in the next section.

Make sure the sub-goals are somewhat specific, so you have something clear to aim for. Losing weight is not a good goal. Losing 5% of body fat or even 15 pounds is a much better goal.

At the end of my list, I write a separate section for smaller, miscellaneous objectives like taking a weekend to hike in Yosemite National Park or visiting Alaska to see the Northern Lights. I try to get to those at some point during the year. (That's why, last year, I saw the Aurora Borealis in -30 degree weather.)

Finally, I write my vision for the year ahead. Some spiritualists believe that if you write it as a vision, the universe will make it so. So I write it as though I'm recapping the year I'm about to live. For example, you may write something like this about the year ahead: "This year, I climbed to the summit of Mt. Kilimanjaro, sold my first business, and found the love of my life."

Make it as detailed as you can, so the universe can work its magic. Even if you don't believe in that, it's a good exercise to get you in the right mindset about accomplishing your goals.

If you don't like writing much, there are plenty of speech-to-text apps. On a Mac, you can even just press the "fn" button twice, and it will allow you to dictate your message to the computer to automatically type for you. It's different for a PC, but there are plenty of apps you can download either way.

Take time over the course of the year to check in on your long-term goals. I like to calendar time once per month to make sure I'm still on track. A few times I've had to course correct. At one point, about halfway through the year, I discovered I had gotten so caught up in business goals that I had let a big personal goal, to take up meditation, fall to the wayside. So right then and there, I signed up for a Transcendental Meditation course and started putting in the work needed to meditate consistently.

GETTING CLEAR ON WHAT MATTERS

For those of you trying to figure out where to even get started on your goal planning, don't worry. I have an exercise to help you. It's one I put to use at the beginning of the year.

Sit down with your calendar, all of your photos from the previous year, and a sheet of paper with two columns labeled "pros" and "cons." Then slowly and thoughtfully scroll through your calendar and photos. Think about the meetings you had, places you visited, work you did, and people you spent time with. List how all of those experiences made you feel. Were they pros or cons in your life? Add each to the proper column.

Write yourself a one-paragraph summary of your desired focus for the coming year, based on those notes. For example, "Spend more time in nature and less time traveling abroad. Spend more time working on projects that help people and less time in meetings that aren't necessary. Say 'no' more."

When I did mine, it suddenly became crystal clear to me where and how I wanted to spend my time in the next year, and with whom. It took me only about 30 minutes. And it was cool to see all the little things I'd done or accomplished that I took for granted.

In setting goals, most people only look ahead and consider what they think they want. This exercise helps you figure out what you want based on real past results. Where you go is powered by where you've been. That's one of the most important lessons you'll ever learn—and the earlier you learn it, the more it compounds.

Choosing a Charity

I'm a firm believer that, if you're making enough to live comfortably, you should be donating to a charity at least once a year. If you don't have the money, volunteer the time. It's a fulfilling and eye-opening experience you can be proud of.

I choose to support Muttville Senior Dog Rescue the most because it's a small organization and I know where my money is going. They often tell me what surgeries they were able to perform on older stray dogs because of my donation, as well as details about their adopters, often military veterans. So I get to help dogs and veterans. (Fun fact: senior dogs are great for military veterans because they're often well trained and just need some love. Some veterans who are disabled don't have the ability to train puppies, so the senior dogs work perfectly.) I also support the ASPCA and any charities that my friends are raising money for throughout the year.

When I was at Udemy, I banded together with two other employees to create Pushup Charity, a competition in which five companies competed in a pushup challenge in costumes in front of an audience for a trophy we had made up. We sold sponsorships to the companies and tickets to the events. All the proceeds went to various local charities the companies selected. In the first two years, we raised over $50,000. You can see more at pushupcharity.org.

It allowed us to give in a big way, even if we personally didn't have a ton of money. It was also fun and allowed us to network with way more CEOs and companies than we normally would've. Selling them on doing a charity event was a lot easier than selling them a product, and it built goodwill along with our personal brands. Most importantly, the charities benefited and it felt great.

At Sales Hacker, we've also run free programs for military veterans fresh out of service to train them in entry-level sales and help them get jobs at tech companies. Find ways to help others and build good karma when you can. It's always worth it.

COLLECT TRAVEL
EXPERIENCES, NOT STUFF

We've discussed how to work when you're traveling. Now let's look at how to make the most of your travel experiences.

I'm a big fan of travel because it gives you chances to learn about other cultures, how to interact with people, how to enjoy being by yourself, and how to get by on a scrappy budget. Travel while you can. Own memories, not things. The more things you own, the more things tend to own you. If you buy a ton of nice furniture, it makes it hard to move or give up your apartment. Staying nimble when you're still trying to figure things out will relieve a lot of stress.

There are few times in your life where you can really get up and go. Once you have a family and kids, or are in the thick of a new company or career, that time will have passed. Do it while you can.

Follow these rules of the road for making travel as smooth as possible:

1. Always book tickets or trips on reputable websites. If the deal looks too good to be true, it probably is. You don't want to learn that the hard way when you get there.

2. As a remote worker, I always inquire in advance about the WiFi at the accommodations I'm staying at and check the reviews for it.

3. When it comes to picking accommodations, value location over amenities almost every time.

4. Use melatonin to fight jet lag and to sleep on overseas flights when you change more than five time zones.

5. Always have some American cash on you and two different typesofcreditcards.Alwayscontactyourbankfirstandletthem know you'll be leaving the country. Stash a $20 bill in your sock if you plan to go out at night or travel to risky areas.

6. If you're backpacking, as I did when I was younger, carry a ski lock with you to lock your bags closed. When necessary, you can even lock them to solid objects.

7. Bring a global socket converter and a small three-headed power strip. You can get these on Amazon or at a local hardware store. It quickly turns one socket into three.

8. Roll your clothes. You'll fit way more. Physics FTW!

9. Bring a drawstring bag to use for day trips while taking up minimal space.

10. Backup your photos over WiFi every day. If you use a cell phone, tether to WiFi and back it up each night. If you have a digital camera, upload nightly, or carry multiple SD cards and swap them out each night. If you lose your camera, you'll only lose that day's photos.

11. Before booking on a travel site, always ask the hotel for a discount via email.

12. Request an upgrade when checking in. It can pay off and can't hurt to ask.

13. Carry a copy of your passport and driver's license when walking around a city, not the actual documents. Leave those at your hotel in a safe for safekeeping.

14. Keep a charged external phone battery in your travel bag at all times.

15. Take a screenshot of important information, including your confirmation numbers for hotel reservations and addresses, before you leave the country. That way when you land, you don't need WiFi or data to access it.

16. I find the $10 per day international plan from Verizon or AT&T to be pretty good when traveling abroad.

17. Pack a few fabric softener sheets in an airtight plastic bag in your suitcase. If you need a quick freshen up, rub one on a shirt and smell like new.

18. Memorize your passport number and keep a pen in a handy compartment of your backpack or travel bag for passport forms.

19. Bring chapstick. It can be surprisingly hard to get in other countries and really expensive.

20. Always practice safe sex! Carry your brand and style with you, as they might not have what you need locally.

READING

Growing up, I hated reading. My parents and teachers couldn't get me to do it. But as I got older, I realized how much I could learn from reading business books. That was part of the inspiration for me to write this one.

I didn't realize back then that there was a playbook for just about everything. There were so many times that I could have learned a great deal by reading up, rather than starting from scratch. Knowing this earlier would have saved me time and heartache.

The key is to find your way to do it—whether through traditional books, e-books, audiobooks on Audible at 3x speed, or even 15-minute summaries on Blinkist. Don't waste time reading tabloids, gossip blogs, or things that may stress you out, like an article about two 26 year olds who just raised a zillion dollars for their company. Just read things that will make you better at what you're looking to achieve.

There are more modern ways to continue learning now like listening to podcasts, taking online courses, and attending conferences. Try them all and figure out what works best for you.

Finding Your Optimal Diet

I'm really into staying in shape. Physical health is important when striving to be your peak self mentally. Exercise is, "one of the most effective ways to improve your mental health," according to *Help-Guide*, a resource on mental and emotional health that collaborates with Harvard Medical School.

Back in college, I used to read fitness magazines. They put out so much content that they'd often contradict themselves. They'd tell you to add raspberries to your diet as they potentially boost your metabolism. Then in the next issue, they'd say to eat less fruit, including berries, because the sugar could turn into fat.

There was no keeping up with it. So in my 20s, I tried some different eating plans.

The one that worked best for me is the Slow Carb Diet, which Tim Ferris wrote about. It involves eating only certain types of vegetables, beans, and meats (except one day a week, when all rules are off and you eat what you want).

The calorie counting with other diets didn't work for me, but this one did. Now, I return to it anytime I want to lose weight. The rest of the year, I eat a more balanced diet, including fruit and some of the meats not allowed in the Slow Carb Diet.

You might find that a different plan works better for you. I've heard good things about Keto, Paleo, and Whole30. And of course, all of this is something for you to discuss with your doctor. I certainly cannot give medical advice, and you should be conscious of how your own body may react to any diet.

I also try to have 30 grams of protein within 30 minutes of waking up. I usually do this with a lean protein shake easy to make with a shaker cup or blender. If I have more time, I'll have a lighter shake and some scrambled eggs with coconut oil. If it's a very busy morning, I'll grab a Quest bar and some almonds.

Alcohol is my vice. In my twenties, I drank often. Now I'm down to a few drinks, two nights per week. If you eat well and get enough sleep, then it's OK to enjoy some alcohol freely.

Your 20s are a great time to experiment and figure out what you like. Be flexible and try it all. Then make it yours. That's how I came to know that my martini order is Ketel One, dry, straight up, olives. My scotch is Lagavulin. My steak order is ribeye, medium rare. Once you've found what you like, don't settle. Ask for it. You deserve it. Own it. People like people who know what they want and know how to ask for it.

But also be ready to give things up. Several years ago, I went cold turkey on another very popular vice: caffeine. Our generation consumes massive sums of it. "Millennials' seemingly unquenchable thirst for coffee is helping to push global demand to a record just as supplies are tightening," *Bloomberg* reported.

I found that caffeine was causing trouble for me. It was worsening my OCD and stomach issues. And for anyone really, excess caffeine just isn't healthy. So I gave it up. Since I was a kid, I've also always been into superfoods. My mom, a yoga teacher and naturopath in New York City, recommended them to me.

My girlfriend has had health struggles, became a certified nutri-tionist, and got into superfoods as well. Together we created SUTRA (www.sipsutra.com), our healthy alternative (or additive) to coffee.

Finding Your Optimal Exercise

If you diet well, you shouldn't need to workout too often to stay in shape. But to stay healthy, exercise is necessary—barring any illnesses that you should discuss with your doctor. To take best care of yourself, I recommend finding a fitness class or routine you can do at least twice a week.

I like to think of a good sweat as a chance to clean out debris from your body. The harder the workout, the faster the blood pumps. Some experts say it helps clear out certain toxins.

I boxed for years in college, but now in my career, it's not so practical. You can't exactly show up for meetings with a black eye or busted nose. These days, I'm a big fan of spin classes, which I can do from anywhere, and yoga for a good stretch and muscle burn.

I also wrote a *Money* column about the benefits I receive from playing hockey. "When I find myself wondering how I'll tackle a huge task, I know it's a good time to go play hockey, which I loved as a kid. While I play, I think back to the days before I knew how to strap on the ice skates and move the puck around. I learned and got good. It reminds me that I can do the same with the task I'm facing at work."

I implore you to find a workout you like and do it at least twice a week.

Getting Your Sleep

"Millennials are the most sleepless generation, with only 29 percent of those between the ages of 18 and 33 saying they regularly get sufficient sleep," *Newsweek* reported.

Some of this has to do with technology. We're more likely than other generations to sleep with our phones right next to the bed. The Pew Research Center found that 83% of Millennials have done so.

Our generation is also stressed. "Both Millennials and Gen Xers report an average stress level of 5.4 on a 10-point scale," the American Psychological Association says. And we're more likely than Gen Xers to say our stress has increased over the past year.

Getting enough restful sleep is incredibly important if you want to fire on all cylinders in your career. Here are key factors to consider:

- **Bed:** Find a good mattress, pillows, and blankets. They are things you'll use almost every day, for six to ten hours per day. And those hours will have a massive effect on what the remaining hours are like. Make them as close to perfect as you can afford.

- **Noise:** If you're living in certain areas of a busy city or with roommates, noise can be tough to cut out at night. I've found that apps such as Calm or Headspace can help. When home, I use the same white noise machine I've used since I was a kid. You can also invest is some really strong noise-cancelling earplugs, but I don't like this because they'll block out emergencies too.

- **Pre-bed habits:** I like to drink Yogi Bedtime or chamomile tea. If I'm hungry, I'll have some almonds and, if necessary, I may take melatonin. It's important to avoid lots of time staring at screens before bed. "The light from our devices is 'short-wavelength-enriched,' meaning it has a higher concentration of blue light than natural light—and blue light affects levels of the sleep-inducing hormone melatonin more than any other wavelength," *Scientific American* explains. I use an app called Flux on my laptop to turn down my computer's blue light. It's synced to go into effect at local sunset.

- **Don't drink late**: Alcohol before bed is a bad idea. "Alcohol literally steals your dreams," *Big Think* explains. It reduces REM sleep, so instead you get "hurtled into a conscious-less void... And we don't even get the benefit from that extra deep sleep, because once the alcohol wears off, those deep sleep phases are so disrupted that the net overall effect is a less restorative night."

- **Blackout**: When I sleep, I like the room to be pitch black. Any light can be detrimental in ways you don't even realize. "Exposure to light in the late evening tends to delay the phase of our internal clock and lead us to prefer later sleep times," Harvard Medical School's Division of Sleep Medicine says. "Exposure to light in the middle of the night can have more unpredictable effects, but can certainly be enough to cause our internal clock to be reset, and may make it difficult to return to sleep."

- **Optimal length**: Some people say getting eight hours is necessary. But the National Sleep Foundation found that the recommended amount for everyone age 18 to 64 is a range, between seven and nine hours. I generally lean toward seven and feel awake and refreshed.

Building Good Habits
& Breaking Bad Ones

All these things I'm suggesting may seem like too much change to make in a short time. But don't think of it that way. Instead, think of a concept called the aggregation of marginal gains, described by British cyclist Dave Brailsford. It's been represented by these two equations:

$$1.01^{365} = 37.8$$
$$0.99^{365} = 0.03$$

The idea is that a 1% improvement each day for a year creates a huge change. But a 1% decrease in performance brings you down to zero really quickly. As venture capitalist Tomasz Tunguz explains on his blog, the theory is a reminder to, "strive to improve each day just a little bit more."

If you've ever tried to change your physique by losing weight or adding muscle, you've probably seen this principle in action. It doesn't happen overnight, but it does happen.

The same is true in your career and at work. Those who are patient, work hard, and focus on getting or doing a bit better day after day will reap the long-term benefits. Like a snowball rolling down hill, you grow a little at a time. The way to do better each day is to take on good habits. They build great careers and even better people.

It's never too late for you to start snowballing. Whatever you do, do it with integrity and purpose. Be whole, undivided, and driven by intention.

Bonus:
Wisdom From Others

Over the course of this book, I've had a lot to say on hacking your career. But of course, I don't have all the answers. So I reached out to successful friends and asked them this question: What's the one thing you wish you knew when you were 22? I've also compiled some of my favorite advice from industry titans and people I've looked up to over the years.

The advice is broken into four categories: learning, earning, growing, and knowing.

On Learning

Jeff Bezos
Founder and CEO, Amazon
"If you're not stubborn, you'll give up on experiments too soon. And if you're not flexible, you'll pound your head against the wall and you won't see a different solution to a problem you're trying to solve."

Daniel Barber
GTM Expert/Consultant for Docusign, Outreach, Chorus, 6Sense
"Understand the value of emotional intelligence. Managers possess the grit and functional skill to succeed, but leaders harness emotional intelligence to develop talent and empower others to achieve their goals."

David Cancel
Co-founder and CEO, Drift (sold four previous companies and is the former CPO at HubSpot)
"There's only one shortcut that will accelerate your career: learning from others. Focus on optimizing your career for learning."

John Barrows
Owner, JBarrows Sales Training (Leading Sales Trainer for Salesforce, Marketo, Box, Zendesk, and LinkedIn)
"When I was 22, the adage of working smart, not hard, didn't connect with me, since I didn't know how to work smart. To work smarter, apply A/B split testing to everything you do. Identify something you want to improve, come up with two different approaches, and see which works better. Then you'll get a lot better a lot faster than I did."

Julie Sokley
VP of Global Sales Operations, AutoDesk
"I wish I knew the importance of getting global experience and learning not only a second language but a third one. Today's millennial bilingual resume is table stakes. But those who are trilingual (or more), or are fearlessly pursuing global projects or roles very early in their careers, are the ones who will advance quickly. Taking a role outside of your home country gives you invaluable experience both personally and professionally."

Trish Bertuzzi
CEO, The Bridge Group, and author of The Sales Development Playbook
"I relied on the company I worked for to educate me and provide me with the training I needed. Silly me. There is a wonderful world of education at our fingertips. I wish I had taken as much advantage then as I do now."

Lesley Young
Global SVP, GM Commercial & Online Sales, Box
"Every role, team, manager, and company presents an opportunity to learn and grow your experience base. Actively push yourself out of your comfort zone and seek out those who have been or done what you haven't to learn from their experience."

Lynne Zaledonis
VP Marketing, Salesforce
"Use your time wisely early on to create a foundation of skill sets that will carry you through a successful and fulfilling career. Be curious."

Matt Cameron
Managing Partner, Frontline Sales (Former VP Global Sales, Yammer)
"Spend as much time as possible with leadership from around your organization to get a deep understanding of the complex organizational processes and politics that drive strategic initiatives and spending. These precious moments were the ones that made the greatest contribution to my success."

Matt Singer
CEO, Videolicious
"Most business processes have some established best practices, and it's possible to move much faster if one can find the right playbook and apply it."

Miles Austin
Sales and Marketing Technologist, Fill the Funnel, Inc.
"Separate your ego from your initiatives and charge forward. Be honest about the causes of your failure, adjust your actions and thinking to correct, and get back at it again. Adjust and refocus, and your actions and your career will reach higher than you can imagine."

Tara Harding
VP of Revenue Ops, HealthVerity
"I wish I had known that I could build the role I wanted, with passion, and not waste time waiting for a company to develop that role. If you can envision, communicate, and show true value in the role you want, go for it!"

Peter Kazanjy
Founder, Modern Sales Salon (former CEO of TalentBin, sold to Monster.com)
"Your career progression is only bounded by your desire and capacity to learn. Do it yourself! It's all about initiative."

Menaka Shroff
Global Head of Marketing, Devices & Mobility, Google
"I was so caught up in getting to the next title or role that I forgot to focus on learning and really understanding my true motivation."

Ralph Barsi
Senior Director of Sales Development, ServiceNow
"Chronicle your experiences and learnings, but share them too. Write and publish. Speak and present. Hear and translate. Do the work—and 'show the work.'"

Richard Harris
Founder, The Harris Consulting Group
"I wish I had stopped to pay attention to what was happening around me from a technology perspective. I wish I'd learned to set and achieve smaller goals as they relate bigger goals and dreams."

Sara Varni
SVP Marketing, Salesforce
"Daily behavior drives long-term success. Find one metric that you can monitor daily and use it as your ongoing progress report."

Rick Nucci
Co-Founder & CEO, Guru (former CEO of Boomi, acquired by Dell)
"Most of the world around you—the things, products, and services—were made by people no smarter than you."

Roderick Jefferson
VP Global Sales Enablement, Marketo
"You're not entitled to anything. You have to earn it. Work as though every opportunity may be your last—and even better, an audition for your next. This will ensure that you're always focused."

Scott Britton
Co-Founder, Troops
"You learn way faster working for all-stars who've run a proven playbook than trying to figure everything out yourself as a young, ambitious person. Be humble and work for someone else to learn to accelerate your growth before you go do your own thing."

Ray Dalio
Chairman & Chief Investment Officer, Bridgewater Associates
"Pain + Reflection = Progress...Mistakes, if you can deal with them the right way, with reflection is where the growth comes from."

ON EARNING

MARK ROBERGE
Former CRO, HubSpot
"Manage your career like your 401K. When you are 22, you invest your 401K in aggressive funds. Similarly, with your career, you should be aggressive. Take risks. Pursue roles where the extent of your responsibilities, financial upside, and potential impact on the world are not dependent on your age or work experience."

LORI RICHARDSON
Sales Accelerator Strategist, Score More Sales
"Compensation is negotiable. I didn't know how to negotiate well. I was happy just to have an opportunity. I made big commissions and received incentive pay but was disappointed later to learn that my salary was less than my male counterparts."

DOUG LANDIS
Growth Partner, Emergence Capital
"Negotiation is a critical skill in your career. You need it to be a great sales rep, as every interaction with a customer is a negotiation. You also need it when getting your career started or moving to a new job. When you're young, you don't really know or understand how to 'value' things like your time, resources, skills, or experience."

JEFFREY GITOMER
Bestselling author (over 1 million books sold)
"Invest, don't spend. My dad and I sold an apartment house and made $100,000 profit in 1969. I spent all the money I got. I didn't understand that winning once didn't ensure winning again."

ON KNOWING

MARC BENIOFF
Founder and CEO, Salesforce
"Realize that you won't be able to bring the same focus to everything in the beginning. There won't be enough people or enough hours in the day. So focus on the 20% that makes 80% of the difference."

AMYRA RAND
VP of Sales, CriteriaCorp
"When I first started working, I let my career manage me instead of the other way around. Eventually, I learned that I had to take ownership of my career and be pragmatic about the roles I accepted and the professional development I pursued."

BLAKE HARBER
Manager of Inside Sales, Lucid Software
"I wish I understood the value of relationships, including the adage that 'your network equals your net worth.'"

EMMANUELLE SKALA
VP of Customer Success, Toast (former VP Sales at many big companies)
"I wish I had learned how to say no. How to prioritize better. How to speak up and not let the BS of work get to me. I wish I took advantage of the time when I had fewer responsibilities and, instead of trying to get ahead, slowed down. Success is not linear and not measured by titles or quota achievement; it's measured by happiness."

KRISTINA McMILLAN
VP of Research, TOPO
"Developing an awareness of those around you is critical to success. Delivering an effective presentation or pitch is important, but it's even more important to be able to 'read the room' and understand how others are receiving your message. Look for cues in body lan-

guage to determine engagement, discomfort, or frustration. Listen to their responses, and try to discern the meaning between the words."

Lars Nilsson
VP Global Inside Sales, Cloudera
"If you don't have somebody inside your company and outside of it that you look up to and trust with your career, then take the time to find that! Invest in these relationships. Set up quick but highly focused 30 minute touch points once a month or quarter."

Jill Rowley
Chief Growth Advisor, Marketo
"I wish I would have known to ask more questions and make more meaningful connections. To be interesting, be interested—in something other than yourself..."

Rob Jeppsen
CEO, Xvoyant
"What I wish I knew at the beginning of my career was how to make a point without making an enemy. This skill has helped me have more influence with people in business and in life."

Kristen Habacht
Head of Enterprise Sales, Atlassian
"It's a real skill to be a good networker and it takes pushing your own comfort zone. Like with any skill, it needs to be practiced and nurtured. It's not just people you have worked with or worked for but also joining new networks."

Anthony Kennada
Chief Marketing Officer, Gainsight
"I wish I fully appreciated at 22 how important the first few jobs out of college actually are—perhaps not in terms of functional experience, but rather, in service of getting great logos on the resume."

On Growing

Simon Sinek
Bestselling Author, Start With Why
"Working hard for something we don't care about is called stress: Working hard for something we love is called passion."

Jack Kosakowski
CEO (US Division), Creation Agency
"If you aren't focused and committed to learning your product, buyer, and industry better than everyone else, you will never be able to achieve your full potential and get yourself to the next level."

Bill Binch
Managing Director, Marketo
"The one thing I wish I knew when I was 22? That I didn't know everything. I thought I did, thought I was right. But I got better with experience and a few laps around the block. Stay hungry, because if you stop learning, that's the moment you start slipping."

Dayna Rothman
CRO, SaaStr
"Stay creative, be motivated, and stay true to yourself. One day, you will have the confidence to command any room!"

Jon Miller
CEO & Co-Founder, Engagio (co-founder and former CMO, Marketo)
"Things are never as good as they seem when times are good, and never as bad as they seem when times are bad. Stay the course and hang in there."

Deidre Moore
Director of Global Marketing, Qstream
"While I was working hard, I was focused on the wrong things and was not listening to good advice. When I was finally able to overcome my stubborn streak, I found success. It's a lesson I still have to remind myself of every now and then, and one that I try to pass along to my team."

Jorge Soto
Co-Founder & CEO, Freedeo
"I wish I would have been more kind to myself, knowing that I was on the right path despite how painful it was at times. You must suffer and recover for the learning to occur. I wish I knew that then."

Lauren Bailey
President, Factor 8
"Chill. It's all going to work out just fine. The hard part is getting that first job. Work hard. Get better every day. Then pay attention to what you love and don't love about it so you can pick your next gigs."

Sam Jacobs
CEO, New York Revenue Collective (Former SVP of Sales & Marketing, Livestream; Former VP Sales, Axial; and Former CRO, The Muse)
"I spent too much time without focus under the assumption that my choices didn't have long-term consequences. What I realized in my 30s is that the secret to success in life is how early you take it seriously. Get humble, start at the bottom, and begin working your way up."

Ursula Llabres
Head of Customer Growth, Workplace by Facebook
"If you do the same thing for 10 years, you will be like a sharp graphite pencil on that one thing. If you vary your experience and the people you work with, including by working with people in different countries, you add depth and breadth to your professional perspective and learn a variety of ways you can have impact. You go

from being a sharp graphite pencil to being a set of polychromos color pencils."

Todd Berkowitz
Managing Vice President, Gartner
"Find a career that you are passionate about and makes you happy. Even if a particular job pays you really well and you like your manager and co-workers, that won't be enough in the long run if you aren't doing something that excites you."

Recommended Resources for Personal and Career Growth

I've come across a few great resources that have helped me along the course of my career. These are a few of my favorites.

Books

The Greatest Salesman in the World, Og Mandino
The 48 Laws of Power, Robert Greene
Start With Why, Simon Sinek
Jab Jab Left Hook, Gary Vaynerchuk
The Four Agreements, Don Miguel Ruiz
The 4-Hour Work Week, Tim Ferris
Ogilvy on Advertising, David Ogilvy
Principles, Ray Dalio
The Tipping Point, Malcolm Gladwell
Sapiens, Yuval Noah Harari
The Fish That Ate The Whale, Rich Cohen
Emotional Intelligence 2.0, Travis Bradberry, Jean Greaves,
    Patrick M. Lencioni
Managing Oneself, Peter F. Drucker
Shantaram (only cause it's awesome), Gregory David Roberts

I asked my LinkedIn following about the books that helped shape their careers. The post was viewed over 70,000 times, and these were the top results.

Meditations, Marcus Aurelius
Never Split the Difference, Chris Voss
How to Win Friends and Influence People, Dale Carnegie
The Alchemist, Paulo Coelho
The 7 Habits of Highly Effective People, Stephen Covey

Biographies & Autobiographies

I find biographies and autobiographies to be some of the best pieces of accessible mentorship that you can find. A few that I recommend are:

Titan: The Life of John D. Rockefeller, Sr., Ron Chernow
Benjamin Franklin: An American Life, Walter Isaacson
I, Steve: Steve Jobs In His Own Words, George Beahm
The Everything Store: Jeff Bezos and the Age of Amazon, Brad Stone
Total Recall: My Unbelievably True Life Story,
   Arnold Schwarzenegger
Shoe Dog: A Memoir by the Creator of Nike, Phil Knight
Snowball: Warren Buffett and the Business of Life,
   Alice Schroeder

ONLINE RESOURCES

The Boron Letters
TheHustle.com
Tim Urban's *Wait But Why*
TED Radio Hour: NPR
Tim Ferriss Podcast and 5 Things Email
Q&As with Warren Buffett (www.buffettfaq.com)
SalesHacker
DigitalMarketer
Copyblogger
Search.FirstRound
Paul Graham Essays
Quora
This Twitter List: twitter.com/hackitmax/lists/career

Personal Technology Stack

These are the technologies I use to power my own life, both personal and business.

Hardware:

- iPhone 8
- A Smart Case battery case on the phone and one spare that's fully charged and ready to go
- Apple AirPods
- 13" Macbook Air with upgraded RAM
- 27" HP monitor for when I'm at my desk and can use the extra screen space
- Apple bluetooth trackpad and keyboard for when I'm at my desk and have the extra screen
- OmniCharge Pro for charging laptops or other gadgets on the go
- Aukey 29W Amp Duo USB wall charger and Apple USB-C charging cord

Software:

- Gmail and Google Docs for email, calendar, and document management
- Slack for communicating with my teams
- Spotify for music
- Google Keep for note taking
- LinkedIn and Instagram for brand building and connecting with my audience
- Twitter, although it's sometimes too noisy
- Quora for learning on the go or before bedtime
- Kindle, Blinkist, and Audible for reading, cliff notes, and audiobooks
- HotelTonight, AirBnb, and Booking.com for travel accommodations

- Foursquare, Yelp, and TripAdvisor for travel help
- TripIt for travel trip tracking
- Lyft or Uber for transportation
- Expensify for expense tracking

A Final
Note From Max

In the end, the best way to learn is by doing. I hope I've given you some things to think about and some guidance on how to set out and make your own mistakes and failures. There's no substitute for that. No reading can replace it, but it can help.

There is no one, single way to do it, so I wish you the best in forging your own path. If you're reading this book, you're already on your way.

If I can do it, so can you.

Good luck.

Acknowledgements

Writing this book was a blast. I wrote my first book, *Hacking Sales*, in six days from the tiny island of Gili Trawangan off Bali, Indonesia. This book was a little different, but not much. I wrote about a third of it in chunks of 1,300 words through LinkedIn posts. I received millions of views on those posts, with thousands of comments on how helpful they were. It was from that feedback that I decided to create this book.

Sections of the book were written from parts of Italy, San Francisco, New York City, the Grand Canyon, Sedona, Miami, the Maldives, and on numerous flights, and was finished over the course of a week back in Bali. This time, from the beaches in Uluwatu and the jungle in Ubud.

Huge thank you goes out to my girlfriend, Ashley, for putting up with me during long silent hours of just me and my computer screen. To my mom, dad, and sister—Karen and David Altschuler and Dina Dori—my number one fans since day one and always did the best they could for me. To my nephews, Evan and Colin, who are inspirations for this book, as hopefully it will be useful for them when they enter the foundation of their careers in a few short years. And to my King Charles Cavalier pups, Brie and Tini, who keep me going through the ups and downs of entrepreneurship and life.

To my fact checker and spiritual guide through this book, Josh Levs; to my editor, Angie Peechatka; and to Gaetano DiNardi, our badass VP of Marketing, who holds down the fort and gives me the opportunity to write a book like this while managing a business. To Joan Mirano, my long-time virtual assistant, who has been with me since my start in tech and whose nieces and nephews call me Uncle Max! And to my teams, both past and present at

Sales Hacker, SUTRA, and all of my other companies, who have worked hard to move mountains with me.

To all of my mentors and people who contributed to my learnings throughout the years, whether they knew it or not. Friends who proofread the book, J. Ryan Williams, Richard Harris, Scott Barker, Jen Spencer, Brad Zomick, Suzanne Rabauer, Howard Kingston, Ryan Buckley, Tawheed Kader, Ralph Barsi. And all our contributors to the Wisdom From Others section.

And most importantly, to everyone who reads this, wants to push themselves, and is motivated to do the best they possibly can, regardless of their circumstances. You inspire me. I was there once, not knowing where it would end up, but as long as you keep pushing, it'll be somewhere good. Trust.

Posing at the park with Intern Brie in
San Francisco

ABOUT MAX

Max Altschuler was born to build things. According to his father, one of his first words was "demolition," which they would say together after spending hours building towers of bricks and knocking them over.

Raised in Syosset, Long Island, Max attended Arizona State University and graduated with a degree in interdisciplinary studies. He has since worked in tech, as an early employee at Udemy, an executive at AttorneyFee (now LegalZoom Local), and the Founder and CEO of Sales Hacker. He's also started or helped build two other multimillion-dollar companies, CMX Media and SaaStr.

Max is a shareholder through investment or advisory in over 40 other startups across the healthcare, agriculture, cybersecurity, sales, marketing, and shipping logistics industries. He recently started a passion project called SUTRA, a superfoods-based healthy coffee alternative that's helping people like him go caffeine-free.

This is Max's second book. His first, *Hacking Sales: The Playbook for Building a High Velocity Sales Machine*, was published by Wiley in 2016 and was an Amazon Bestseller. A widely recognized thought leader, he has been published by *The Harvard Business Review, Money, Inc., Forbes,* and many other outlets.

When Max isn't building companies, helping people with their careers, or writing, he spends time traveling around the world and working from different locations. At time of writing, he has visited more than 80 countries. He lives and travels with his girlfriend, Ashley, and their dogs, Brie and Tini.

LinkedIn: linkedin.com/in/maxaltschuler
Twitter: @HackItMax
Instagram: @HackItMax
Personal Site: www.maxalts.com
Career Hacking: www.getcareerhacking.com
Sales Hacker: www.saleshacker.com
SUTRA: www.sipsutra.com

In the studio at Salesforce HQ

Working remotely from this week's poolside office

Presenting at a conference in front of 5,000+ Sales and Marketing Professionals in Brazil

CAREER HACKING NOTES

Made in the USA
San Bernardino, CA
25 May 2018